DATE DUE

Brands L

Brands Laid Bare

Using Market Research For Evidence-based Brand Management

Kevin Ford

John Wiley & Sons, Ltd

Other Wiley Editorial Offices

John Wiley & Sons Inc., 111 River Street, Hoboken, NJ 07030, USA

Jossey-Bass, 989 Market Street, San Francisco, CA 94103-1741, USA

Wiley-VCH Verlag GmbH, Boschstr. 12, D-69469 Weinheim, Germany

John Wiley & Sons Australia Ltd, 33 Park Road, Milton, Queensland 4064, Australia

John Wiley & Sons (Asia) Pte Ltd, 2 Clementi Loop #02-01, Jin Xing Distripark, Singapore
129809

John Wiley & Sons Canada Ltd, 22 Worcester Road, Etobicoke, Ontario, Canada M9W 1L1

Wiley also publishes its books in a variety of electronic formats. Some content that appears in
print may not be available in electronic books.

British Library Cataloguing in Publication Data

A catalogue record for this book is available from the British Library

ISBN 0-470-01283-8 (hbk)

Typeset by Dobbie Typesetting Ltd, Tavistock, Devon
Printed and bound in Great Britain by Antony Rowe Ltd, Chippenham, Wiltshire
This book is printed on acid-free paper responsibly manufactured from sustainable forestry
in which at least two trees are planted for each one used for paper production.

Contents

Preface

This book paints a picture of how brands work from the consumer's point of view – a perspective increasingly important as branding moves away from 'marketing at people' towards a more equal relationship with people. The book describes how people experience brands and choose between them. It lays a lot of emphasis on understanding people's needs, it explains and demystifies terms such as brand equity and loyalty, and it looks at indications of brand success in the future.

It draws on 20 years' experience of conducting market research studies on behalf of my clients, the owners and managers of brands. Indeed, the practising market researcher is in the unique position of being asked to study objectively the interaction between people and brands. It means the observations in this book are either direct findings from research studies, or extrapolations from patterns seen repeatedly over many studies. I believe this empirical foundation gives the book its strength. It will also provide a contrast to most other books that talk about brands. They often provide a compelling vision of what makes a brand successful, including persuasive case histories, but their perspective tends to come across as 'what marketing tries to do to people'. The researcher's tale favours the other side of the coin, emphasising what we have seen in terms of consumer response, and placing less weight on the marketing intentions.

Anyone involved in brands, marketing and business in general will find the book helps them better understand their customers. It will help inform marketing strategy, in the light of the growing enthusiasm for 'customer-centric marketing', and it will interest market researchers, who will find new insights as well as points in common with their own experience.

But, do note that this book is *not* about research technique. Its subject is the lessons learned about people and brands, derived from research studies. In some places I have found it helpful to mention some points about technique, but only to clarify the basis of the findings. In particular, I have drawn attention to the good research techniques that underpin some of the key issues in the book. I am well aware that people unfamiliar with research may be concerned that much of it is based on crude, direct questions. This is not the case.

There are also some areas where I have challenged the conclusions of others, for important technical reasons, all of which are explained as clearly as possible. That said, I have kept all technical comment to a minimum.

My research experience began with the research agency RSL in the UK, and then continued within the Ipsos Group, following their acquisition of RSL in 1992. Ipsos is one of the largest world-wide survey-based research groups, and this has provided me with access to large amounts of knowledge, expertise, case histories and research and development work from across the world. It also includes many companies acquired by Ipsos over the past few years, each of whom has brought a slightly different set of research techniques and experiences. And in addition, I spend time studying the work of many other research agencies!

Putting all this together, I have placed most weight in this book on findings that crop up repeatedly, even when different research techniques have been applied. That sort of consistency, particularly where it seems accidental, gives us reason to believe that the conclusion is reliable.

There will, of course, be many researchers out there who have a different story to tell, or who feel I have not gone into enough depth on some important topics. I encourage them to write their own books, and add to our developing picture of brands.

Acknowledgements

I would like to thank the many people who have helped contribute ideas and support for this book. This includes a wide range of people throughout Ipsos, the global research company where I work, as well as my clients and others working in brand management.

In particular, I owe special thanks to:

John Hallward, for his exceptional knowledge of brand equity, and the time he has spent helping to refine the ideas presented in this book;
Mike Denny, for his ability to see through to the essence of ideas, and suggest better ways of presenting them; and
Katherine Page, for her advice on language and style, and her constant support during the writing of the book.

1

What do People Want from a Brand?

Introduction

The way we relate to brands has changed. In the middle of the twentieth century, brand management was about using marketing 'to do things to people'. The people were collective rather than individuals, the emphasis was on the brand's marketing, and choices were made by the brand manager, not by the customer. Now there is a wave of new marketing that is shifting the focus towards the customer. It talks about greater equality with consumers, empowering them to make their own choices, treating them as thinking individuals rather than an amorphous mass. Doubtless this paints too extreme a picture, but the general direction is evident.

A consequence of this trend is an increased interest in understanding people, as a foundation for marketing brands. This is where the market researcher comes in. Over the past 20 years I have experienced a growth of demand for research into consumers' needs and their attitudes to brands, and this forms the subject of this book: how to look after a brand, based on understanding people.

Taking the customer as the focal point, we begin by looking at their associations with a brand – all the content they carry around about a brand, knowingly or unknowingly. This provides the foundation for going deeper into understanding people's needs, and how these relate to brands. For example, many telecommunications brands tap into a deep human need for connecting with other people. This shows the role which a brand can play in someone's life and, at a deep level, the reason why they want it.

Moving from, 'Why would I be interested in it?' to, 'How well does it do its job?', we will look at how people make overall judgements about a brand. This is not just one total assessment, but covers a small number of key measures that summarise the level of desire for a brand, for example how people rate its quality, the extent to which they feel it offers something different, and the clarity of what it stands for. These overall judgements we call *brand equity*.

That covers the what and why. We then look at *how* a brand does this through various points of contact with people, which we term the 'touchpoints' between the person and the brand. And from a different slant, we go on to discuss targeting: which types of people in which types of situations.

But desire for a brand is not enough. Many brands successfully distinguish themselves from other brands, but fail to convert these positive qualities into sales. We identify the factors that make the link between brand equity and brand sales. And finally we tackle the most difficult topic: exploring the ups and downs of brand success.

Brand Associations

Think about a specific brand. Try to identify all the associations you have with that brand, all the situations, emotions, memories, images, colours, smells and so on. This is a difficult task, and a core skill of the market researcher is to have techniques for tackling this in conversations with people.

Imagine we are discussing a brand of coffee with someone. Some of the associations we may discover might be:

- the sound when piercing the foil of a new jar, and the sense of freshness and warm aroma that comes out;

- a strong, bitter taste, that gives you a slight kick when you take the first sip;
- an aging relative, Aunt Mildred, who always offered you a cup of this brand when you went to visit her;
- being in an office, unable to make progress on your work until you have a cup to pick you up;
- a vague impression of exotic places where the beans are grown;
- a famous actor who has advertised the brand;
- your neighbour, who drinks the brand;
- oranges (next to the coffee jar on your shelf).

These associations generate various reactions. They may induce a neutral response or strong feelings, either drawing you emotionally towards the brand or repelling you. They may invoke action and energy, or calm and stability. They may lead to rational assessments about the brand, for example, 'I want that particular feature that is offered by the brand'. And they may strengthen a sense of continuity or habit, if the associations are long-standing and reinforced through repeated experiences and consistent marketing.

Some of these associations, such as the famous actor, will be common to all people that have noticed them. Other associations will be more specific to the individual, such as Aunt Mildred. But many of those may be part of a shared experience to a certain extent, since many people may have someone like an Aunt Mildred, even if their own version has slightly different characteristics. And there will be some apparently random associations, that result from an accident of the individual's experience – they may keep the coffee jar next to the oranges in their own home.

Even when associations are common to many people, reactions to those associations will vary. The association may be essentially objective, such as, 'this coffee is made from pure arabica beans', but the way people react to that information will depend on their own motivations and the type of person they are. One person will find it exotic, stimulating and pleasurable, while another may find it elitist, distancing and difficult to understand. And in many cases the associations can be contradictory within the same individual. Aunt Mildred, the famous actor and the person's neighbour may all trigger very different reactions, some positive and some negative.

Having said that, the associations that influence brand choice most powerfully are those that are shared by many people and which evoke a consistent positive meaning. These are often based on some association with an identifiable aspect of the brand's marketing, such as a specific product or service feature, or a mood or image consistently conveyed by the brand (such as humour).

The general task of the market researcher is to identify and make sense of these associations and perceptions. We tend to focus more on the common associations and major themes that will help a brand manager, but we also recognise the uniqueness of each individual's story. And we are a lot more subtle than some people realise.

We rarely ask people directly *why* they buy something. Direct questions tend to evoke responses that are overly rational, and limited to aspects that sound acceptable to admit publicly. People are more inclined to say they buy a brand because it tastes delicious, than to admit they are influenced by the pretty packaging. To avoid this we use more indirect techniques, such as asking people to describe their overall preference between different brands, as well as asking for their detailed associations with the brand and their perceptions of what it does well and poorly. We then infer which aspects are important, by observing which perceptions and associations connect strongly with the preferred brand.

Good researchers are alert to the pitfall that normal language can sound very objective. The phrase 'that brand tastes delicious' runs the risk of sounding like an objective fact, or the judgement of a panel of expert tasters whose opinions will be accepted as the truth for all of us. In this case it is easy to see that taste is a subjective judgement by each individual, but it even applies to apparently more factual issues, such as the luggage space in a car. We can read about factual measures of the load capacity, but our perceptions are still subjective, influenced by softer issues such as how easy it looks (to us) to fit things in, and specific personal experiences.

People don't make scientific judgements comparing brands on a fair and equal basis. They draw conclusions, often subconsciously, based on the accidental intersection of the brands and their lives.

Typically, market researchers study many brands that compete in a 'category', and Figure 1.1 (see overleaf) shows a 'map' of some brand perceptions you might find for the coffee category.

In these sorts of maps, the perceptions are positioned according to their meaning. In quantitative research studies, these positions are determined by the patterns in the data. For example, 'full-flavoured' and 'aromatic' appear close together, since brands are broadly perceived to have both characteristics or to have neither of them. Conversely, 'energised' and 'quiet and relaxed' appear far apart on the map, since most brands tend to emphasise one or the other association, but rarely manage both. We will talk more later about the shape of this map, when we discuss general themes of consumer needs.

Many themes are discernible in each area of the map. For example, a particular brand may emphasise an 'energy' theme, through an emphasis on perceptions appearing on the left side of the map. It may be perceived to have a strong taste, deep rich colour, be good for active situations, making you feel full of life and energy, and it says to other people that you are a dynamic, go-ahead sort of person. If you are aiming to build your brand on this theme, then working via all these sorts of perception will contribute to the total effect.

Different perception items do not act independently of each other in driving desire for a brand. A soft texture to the product is likely to contribute to an association with feelings of gentleness. And a common mistake is to assume that functional perceptions will contribute to emotional reactions, but it can also be the other way round. You may convey a sense of heritage and seriousness for a brand, which influences people's perception of how it tastes. People may well perceive it to have more body and depth than they would if it did not carry those emotional connotations. A good example is evident for many brands of whisky. They carry a strong perception of 'authenticity', deriving from tangible qualities of the process of production and maturing, as well as from more emotional aspects concerning the traditions of the specific location associated with the brand.

Energised

Out with friends

Sophisticated

Excited
Early morning

Good times
Discerning
Dinner party

Full-flavoured

Dynamic

Real hit
Dark
Aromatic
Happy
Friends around

Full-bodied

Confident
Light
Mellow

At work
Mild

Home by self
Fitting in

Strong
Bitter
Intelligent
Quiet and relaxed

Ordinary

On top of things
Receptive
Down to earth

Figure 1.1 Perceptions for the coffee category

Consumer Needs

What is a Need?

As we identify themes from groups of perceptions, we move towards deeper consumer needs. This is illustrated by Figure 1.2 (see overleaf).

The figure shows an example of a supermarket. At the top level are listed a number of specific perceptions, such as convenient location, short checkout queues, and so on. Below these we have identified two themes. The three attributes of convenient location, efficient staff and short checkout queues all contribute to making a shopping trip faster, so they combine into a theme of speed. The family parking, range of trolley types and toilets are all facilities which help make the trip easier, or more comfortable. So we have two themes, speed and ease, which we have then combined on the lowest level into one major synthesis of 'practicality'.

A spectrum is apparent. The items on the top level are very specific perceptions that seem closely linked to the brand. The synthesis at the bottom level is much broader; it gets down to deeper needs, and it is very much about the person.

Technically we should probably be more cautious about the use of the word 'needs'. This word should be reserved for aspects of human life which are involuntary and inescapable, and many psychologists have worked to show that there are very few such things. However, there is an opposite drawback with using other words such as 'motivations' or 'drives'. These tend to sound much more like questions of choice, and seem to be a little weak for the 12 aspects we have labelled as needs later in this section. So we will stick with 'needs', recognising that it is not perfect but we hope that it is well understood in this context.

The top level includes attributes which are very specific to the current concerns and ways of running a supermarket (e.g. different types of trolley), but themes on the second level are generally independent of market structure and the mechanisms through which brands deliver the service or the product. The need for speed in our dealings with service brands is a characteristic of modern life which would remain even if the mechanisms changed radically. For example, the introduction of the self-scanning

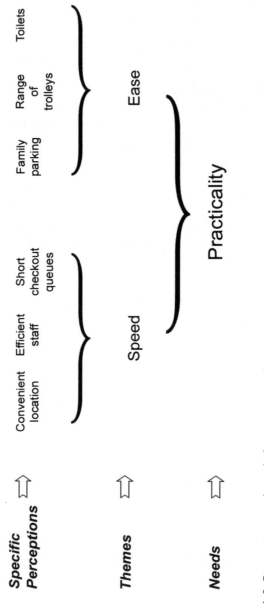

Figure 1.2 Perceptions and needs for a supermarket

system has removed the checkout issues from the equation, but the need for speed remains.

So themes such as speed and ease, which sit on this second level, are arguably much more useful to focus on. They allow you to think outside the framework of the existing market structure, and explore ways in which new mechanisms for your product or service might benefit the consumer. They also enable you to compare very different sorts of brands, particularly in service industries. The mechanisms for meeting the need for 'convenience' of a banking service will be very different for Internet banking and for branch-based banking, but the convenience need will be highly relevant in both cases.

You might reasonably suggest stopping at level two, but you can go a step further to fundamental human needs. Here we are talking about things which relate to the human condition, potentially nothing to do with the world of brands. A sense of order or structure would be an example for this level, while 'speed' would not. To the best of my knowledge, no psychologist has ever suggested that the human organism has a fundamental need for speed, but they all include something to do with deep feelings like love and belonging.

A way of seeing these distinctions in action is to keep asking why, every time you say someone has a certain need. So, people need efficient staff in shops (top level), because they have a broader or deeper need for speed (middle level), in turn because they have a fundamental need for practicality (lowest level).

This cascading quality points to the idea of being able to do without some things at the higher levels, while you cannot do without the needs at the deepest level. You can do without the efficient staff if there is another way of making the total shopping experience fast. And speed is a less powerful concept in your life than the need for practicality. This implies that brands will be most successful if they tap directly into the most fundamental human needs. They will also be successful, though less so, if they aim for the second level, since these are slightly more a 'means to an end'. And they certainly shouldn't concentrate only on one or two first-level items, since the benefits those provide could be overtaken by competitors using other mechanisms.

Note that the importance of each need is not usually constant for each individual. Speed may be crucial on one shopping trip, while some other aspect such as menu suggestions for a dinner party may be more important on another trip. This increased variability is a general trend, as our lives become less governed by routine and as the availability of choices increases.

You might ask why a brand should try to touch a fundamental human need, when people do not look to brands to fulfil all their needs. Someone might, for example, get their sense of peace and harmony from long walks in a forest, nothing to do with brands. The answer is that a brand's marketing is most successful if it manages to tap into our fundamental needs, and there is no barrier to brands doing this. It's a somewhat frightening observation, but there seems to be no area of life untouched by brands. They may play a supporting role rather than a leading one, but it is evident that brands can aim at any human need. Some may argue that this enriches life, while others may be concerned that it risks replacing a different and better way of living. Either way, brands have the opportunity to aim for these primary human needs, whatever they are.

Major Themes of Needs in the Coffee Example

Figure 1.3 shows the coffee perceptions map, with suggestions of 12 fundamental needs arranged around the circle. These are my suggestions for a core list which can usefully be applied to the analysis of any category or brand. The reason for proposing a list of 12, and the distinction between the needs identified in capital letters and those in lower case, will be discussed in the next section. For now, let's get familiar with each of these themes through a practical example.

Starting at the bottom of the map, we have the need for Structure. This corresponds with situations which require some sense of control or organisation. Moving to the left, it shades into the need for Practicality, so it covers situations such as being at work, the expression of intelligence, and feeling on top of things. This moves into the need for Challenge, connecting with product characteristics of strength and bitterness, and a

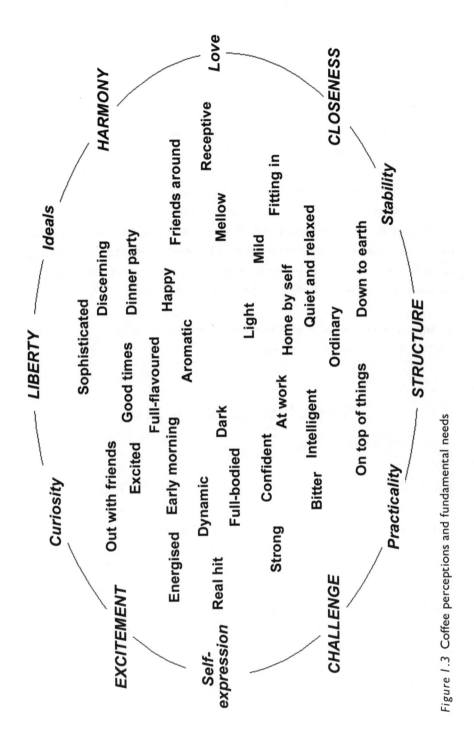

Figure 1.3 Coffee perceptions and fundamental needs

sense of confidence or achievement. Moving further round, we come to Self-expression, encompassing the direct expression of energy and dynamism, a full-bodied product that gives you a feeling of get-up-and-go. Next we come to the need for Excitement, still expressing energy but with more of an upbeat lift and having fun, perhaps in a situation such as being out with friends. And this merges into Curiosity, the need to explore and discover, looking for new experiences.

At the top of the chart we have the need for Liberty, placed opposite the need for Structure. This is about freedom and openness, the unexpected rather than the routine. This then moves into the need for Ideals, including refinement, sophistication and discernment, and situations such as a dinner party with style as a high consideration. This shades into Harmony, feelings of being happy, and perhaps having a friend or two around, then the need for Love, feeling receptive and supportive. This continues into Closeness, meaning the desire to fit in, feel protected and secure. Then Stability, feeling quiet and relaxed in a familiar environment, at home by yourself. And finally we come back to Structure.

The Universal Needs Map

Description of the Map

The 12 universal needs are shown in Figure 1.4, with three major pairs identified by the arrows. These should be viewed as complementary, not opposites. Indeed, we will see how successful brands frequently manage to encompass both components within a complementary pair.

The labels for these 12 needs have been developed through conducting a great number of research studies, seeing reports of many others, and absorbing a large body of literature on the subject. Other words could be suggested for these needs, but it is the underlying concept in each case that is most important, not the precise word.

The shape of the map, with its major themes, appears consistently across categories. I have seen dozens, perhaps hundreds, of such maps, produced from surveys where the designer had no intention of controlling the

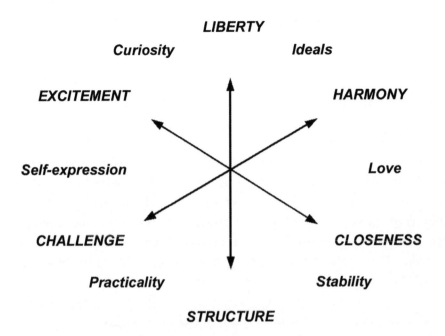

Figure 1.4 The universal needs map

outcome of the mapping. The shape has always been broadly the same. Sometimes it varies slightly, though this is usually explicable by the precise items that have been included. Typically, you find that a research study has incorporated a large number of items relating to the main areas of emphasis in a category, and relatively fewer items in areas that are currently less relevant to the category. This means that those maps are sometimes slightly distorted versions of the universal map, though the themes are there if you look.

It is a very important point that the shape occurs naturally, rather than just being imposed from a theory. This emphasises the importance of the framework we are describing, and it also explains why many different researchers and research companies have developed variations along the same lines. It is very likely to appear like this.

There are alternative types of map that lay out the main themes in different positions relative to each other. This can be useful for exploring interesting marketing strategies, and I am sure they would provide further insight about a category, but they do not occur empirically, or at least not with the same frequency as this universal map.

The map can be rotated or flipped over. Indeed, when computer programs are run to generate these maps they can come out with any orientation. Liberty may come out at the top, the bottom, the left or the right-hand side.

Conventionally, most people place Liberty at the top and Structure at the bottom of the page (or their equivalents of these concepts). The reason for this seems to be a widely-held association of Liberty with concepts that are viewed positively by the Western world, including freedom, extraversion, progress and youth. Structure relates to some concepts which are viewed negatively, such as repression, control, intraversion and old age. This is unfortunate, since it misses many positive qualities that should be connected with Structure, though it seems this may be changing. For example, we see a growing interest in the UK in the provenance of food, which connects with this need to understand origins.

There is less consistency about left and right. I am personally most familiar with seeing the Excitement/Challenge groupings on the left and the Harmony/Closeness groupings on the right, but many people would swap them over. It really doesn't matter. The important point is that the *adjacencies* of the needs are consistent: Liberty next to Ideals, next to Harmony, next to Love and so on.

There is no magic about the number 12. The number of fundamental needs you identify is largely a matter of personal choice. You can break them down into a larger number if you prefer, or you can reduce them to a smaller number. Practically, a system with fewer than around six becomes too broad and conceptual to be very helpful, while a system with more than around 15–20 is too detailed. By this stage you will tend to have some detailed 'sub-needs' which group together into some 'broader needs'. The number 12 does, however, have considerable advantages when we compare the many different approaches to this subject in the literature. It makes it easier to identify connections and illustrates an underpinning of this needs framework in many diverse areas of human life and thought. It also provides a flexibility of interpreting patterns, since it can usefully be aggregated into two, three, four or six groups.

In fact, among all the possible choices of numbers, there are three 'families'. There is a family based on the numbers 3, 6 and 12, including the system we have suggested. There is another based on the numbers 2, 4, 8 and possibly 16. And there is a third family, which is usually based on an odd number such as 5 or 13. The first two talk about dimensions and opposites, while the third approach is typically a simple list, though it can be arranged around the circle on our universal map. There is no right or wrong; all of the systems are potentially valid and lead to the same conclusions. In the next section we will first describe the universal map and the 3/6/12 family, and then comment on extra perspectives from the other approaches.

Before doing so, we should point out some of the potential pitfalls of interpretation in any of these approaches, particularly those which emphasise dimensions and opposites. This appears to imply that a brand has a choice between conflicting alternatives. For example, the assertion that you can be practical, or you can be idealistic, but you can't achieve both. This is misleading. Many of the most successful brands are able to combine apparent opposites, rather than being trapped into meeting one need at the expense of another. For example, we might suggest that Coca-Cola emphasises excitement and liberty, but at the same time conveys a comforting familiarity and timelessness, so fitting the needs of structure and closeness. McDonalds expresses a personality of strength and control, so emphasising challenge and the left side of the map, but it also stresses a lot of sharing and family situations, hence also the right side of the map.

This pattern corresponds with wide relevance for successful brands, able to meet many contrasting needs, while at the same time emphasising certain needs very effectively and uniquely. Strong niche brands, on the other hand, make their name on one or two types of needs, but often at the expense of the opposite types of needs. When you imagine a brand 'positioned' in the map, it is too limiting to think of a 'centre of gravity', shown as a point on the map. For brands like Coke and McDonalds, this risks being placed near the middle, hiding their strength of meeting contrasting needs. It is better to use some kind of representation that shows the strength of the brand on each need.

Three major pairs or dimensions, covering six needs, are shown in the universal map.

- *Excitement-Closeness* covers a dimension ranging from expansion, potential and confidence, through to safe, emotional security within comforting boundaries.
- *Liberty-Structure* is the contrast of freedom and exploration of anything new, through to structure, control and anchorage in forms.
- *Harmony-Challenge* is the choice between balance, equality and sharing, versus winning, overcoming, seeing the self as important and above others instead of equal to others.

These three dimensions and six needs have been picked out above the others. A strong case can be made for listing them all with equal weight, but we will see the major list occurring in other approaches to exploring human needs.

Now let's go through each of the 12 needs in turn, studying its meaning in more detail and identifying examples of brands and product or service categories that connect strongly with them.

Structure

This need is about groundedness, holding everything together, a need for things to be well organised and under control. It is the virtue of routine and a systematic approach. It obviously relates to the physical body, and the physiological needs of hunger and thirst, as well as a psychological need to be able to 'see the wood for the trees'. On a higher level, it can be about seeing a world order, where we have come from and where we are going. On a mundane level, food and drink categories therefore satisfy the hunger element of this need. They can do this not just in a negative, problem-removal way, but also in a positive way, tapping the growth of awareness of good ingredients and the *appreciation* of food quality, as well as its enjoyment. On the next level any brand which helps you to organise your life, such as the filofax or Psion organiser, is tapping this need. And, more connected with the world order theme, look at the growing appetite for history and popular science, including interest in genealogy, connections and roots.

In terms of operation, any brand which is clear and straightforward in everything it does will connect with this need. This has often been viewed in the past in a negative way, with terms such as 'basic' and 'ordinary', or euphemisms such as 'down to earth'. But in a world of increasing complexity, there are opportunities for brands which keep it clear and simple. Let's imagine a brand called *Foolproof*, offering absolutely reliable products or services, with the concisest of usage instructions, which work every time regardless of how tired you are. This brand never offers you alternatives, fresh ideas or emotional support, but you know exactly where you stand with it.

Practicality

This is about getting the job done, skill and efficiency. It also covers physical expression and experience, a celebration of the senses and the physical world. In a world increasingly connected by technology and speed, we still require a groundedness with our physical form – witness the success of health and fitness clubs.

A specific brand which springs to mind is Nike. In fact Nike taps into a broader range of needs in the bottom left corner of the map since it includes a sense of challenge as well as physicality. Its advertising has illustrated the joy of physical expression, the swoosh (tick) shape of its logo has an appropriate directness about it, and the slogan 'just do it' captures the spirit of challenge and getting on with it. Most brands involved with sport are likely to operate in this area, but Nike seems to tap it better than most.

Another example is Ronseal, with its iconic slogan 'It does exactly what it says on the tin', delivered assertively in the advert by a no-nonsense personality. It makes a perfect connection with the need for practicality, by reassuring you that practicality is its whole focus: it does it, it does it exactly, and you know what it does because it tells you.

So more broadly, we find this is the area of engineering quality and effective industry and technology. This can take the form of 'harsh, real world', or it can be somewhat more prestigious, for experts who are 'in the know'. The Audi slogan 'Vorsprung durch Technik' (advantage through technology) neatly captures the connection between this need and the progressive open-minded spirit of Liberty. Indeed, science at its most effective combines the top and the bottom of the needs map. The top is all about ideas, while the bottom is all about making them work: the combination of pure and applied mathematics.

Challenge

This covers a number of sub-themes. It is the urge to achieve, to succeed, to take up a challenge such as climbing Everest, just because it is there. In this sense there does not need to be direct reference to an opponent, or other people. It can be a very personal sense of achievement. Think of something like the desire to run a marathon, and brands which promise you the energy to run faster and jump higher or further. It is also competitive: the urge to beat an opponent, so obviously a lot of sport falls into this need. This urge for victory can extend to a power over others, the expression of authority and status or prestige. This is the more extrovert, publicly visible side of Challenge. When you think of cars, you are likely to associate brands such as Mercedes and BMW with this sort of need: the choice of people who are affluent and successful, with a brand that indicates their status.

There is an important distinction here. The Challenge need expressed through status is not about the refinement of glamour, seduction and charm. That belongs more in the upper right part of the map, as a form of Ideal. What we find with Challenge, in the lower left area of the map is often much cruder. It can be 'big business', with all the subtlety of a juggernaut. It is capable and successful. When Challenge is combined with the Practicality need, it is the triumph of substance versus style, expressed through Ideals and Harmony.

In a reversal of status, but still relating to the Challenge need, we find vengeance. While we love prestige and celebrity, we also love its antithesis, so we like to see people get their comeuppance. The tabloid press provide vengeance against celebrities, while many TV programmes delight in humiliating ordinary people as well as the rich and famous. And so it can be the rebel, with or without a cause.

Another expression of the Challenge theme is the positioning of certain cold and flu remedies, those which attack the cold and flu with maximum force, allowing you to carry on and meet life's challenges, whether this is your boss's demands at work or anything else. This sort of positioning, certainly when combined with the Practicality need, seems at first sight to be the obvious one for many products. Your expectation might be that we have very wide-ranging needs from *services*, so that might reasonably include all parts of the map, but that *products* are simpler and focused more toward the practical delivery, lower-left area of the map. This is not the case. Many cold and flu remedies aim for the opposite to Challenge, emphasising harmony and closeness. They take the approach of gently soothing the problem away, caring for you and telling you it's OK to give in to it. They work on your feeling needs.

Self-expression

This need is all about self, discovering and asserting your identity, so it emphasises ego, strength and independence. It means doing it your own way for the sake of it, regardless of whether that is better than another way.

Here, brands and products that help us to do our own thing tap into this need. This might be empowerment as a customer of a service, such as financial products that can be tailored to what we want. There was an advert for the Midland Bank (pre-HSBC) a few years ago. A customer, intelligent, confident and assertive, but also fair and reasonable, goes to see his bank manager. The manager has a couple of colleagues as back-up, but is effortlessly overpowered by the customer. He tells the manager what characteristics he wants from his bank account, and the manager has no choice but to listen and accept it. This may not seem very revolutionary today, but my memory is that it expressed 'customer-power' in a striking way at the time. By contrast, many competitive brands emphasise the opposite need about caring for their customers and being nice, ethical companies.

There is a great opportunity here for brands of the future, which allow the customer to make choices. The recipe seems to work best today if you give the customer a template of fairly limited parameters to play with, enough to *feel* that they have expressed their own choices, without necessarily giving them a blank sheet of paper.

The Self-expression need can also be tapped by any brand that makes us feel strong and independent. This could be self-help books, DIY products, and so on.

Another example of a slogan which fits here is L'Oreal's 'Because you're worth it'.

Excitement

This is about getting out there and living life, upbeat emotions, high energy, having fun. Think of something like bungee jumping, followed by a party with loads of drink, meeting new people, and then exploring the consumption of Haagen-Dazs ice cream with a new partner. It is confident, extroverted and high-adrenaline: think high-energy recreation such as Club 18–30 holidays, or paintballing. Indeed, it often conjures up situations involving large groups of people. When you study the market for social drinking, this is where you find upbeat events, partying on Friday and Saturday nights. And this is where the big money is spent, so it is a lucrative target for the major brands, such as Carling or Fosters. Notice the traditional emphasis on humour and fun for these brands, and the care to portray large groups, more than just a couple of people. The Excitement need can sometimes be connected to one individual, but it seems to work most often with groups, team sports and activities rather than individuals.

It is also the area of taking risks and spinning the wheel of fortune, so this would be fruitful ground for brands such as the National Lottery, selling the excitement of the possibility of winning. Hence, it is also very future-oriented, and frequently geared to youth culture.

Curiosity

This is about learning and growth, curiosity for its own sake. It is more about ideas than about energy. It is the desire to discover and find out;

particularly a mental need, rather than the need for experience. The perfect example of a brand tapping this need is Microsoft, using the name Explorer for its Internet package and the slogan, 'Where do you want to go today?'. Think also about anything to do with education. Everyone's at it these days, through evening classes, books, online learning, part-works series, idiot's guides to this and that, and so on. We all want to know what's going on.

A brand trying to tap this need would educate and stimulate curiosity, being careful to hint at new discoveries to be made along the way, not revealing too early everything that is to come.

Liberty

This is the pure opposite to Structure, a rising above all constraints, a sense of total possibility and new things. It relates strongly to modernity in all forms. This is where you find fashion, always looking for what is new and what is 'in', even if this means recycling something old in a new form, just to avoid repetition. It is the urge to have the latest thing, the latest gadget.

Obviously it's hard work for a brand to consistently tap this need, unless it evolves and changes constantly, which is possible but hard going. It would need to be a brand constantly reported in the news for confounding expectations – just when you expected them to do this, they did the opposite. It means a brand which becomes associated with constant innovation and invention.

Another aspect of Liberty is the need for *escape*: anything which breaks the familiar routine, or takes you out of your normal environment. Anything to with travel, hobbies, leisure pursuits or a change of scene fits here. It is spontaneous and open to anything, whereas the opposite need of Structure fits with planning and knowledge in advance of all possible outcomes.

Ideals

This need operates on many levels, both on a private and public basis. On one level, the meaning of Ideals translates into refinement: glamour and seduction, sophistication and elitism. Think of a brand such as Sheba cat food, where the cat is a sophisticated, almost unattainable lover, to be wooed and worshipped.

On another level this is about good causes, the desire for a sense of community and responsible progress, asking the questions, 'Where are we going?' and 'What can I do to be a part of that?' This is a refinement of principle, as opposed to a refinement of style. Brands that catch this need are asking you to act on principle, rather than on practical considerations. Good examples would be the Body Shop, with its support for fair and ethical sourcing of materials, and the Co-Op Bank. You might also think of organic foods, and 'movement' brands such as Greenpeace.

There is also a private, spiritual development side to the need for ideals. This could mean activities such as yoga or the creation of art, and any brand that helps you realise a sense of personal fulfilment. This tends to shade into the Harmony need as well, since many of these things imply discovering a sense of inner peace.

Harmony

This is a big need, a counterpoint to the opposing need for Challenge. Here we are looking at appreciating other people, their viewpoints and their feelings. It can be connected to a sort of gracious living, where politeness and etiquette are given a high priority. We are talking courtesy, friendliness and adaptability to others. Taken with the neighbouring need of Ideals, this is all about *style*, contrasting with the *substance* found in the opposite corner of the map.

Again we find that this need, like the others, can be expressed on many levels. It can be external, about your dealings with others, in which case we are looking at brands which emphasise that they are 'nice to do business with', particularly service brands. It also has a more internal aspect, directed to a sense of inner peace. This can be an antidote to the fast, stressful pace of life, expressed through such brands as *The Little Book of Calm* or Prozac. It can also be something more holistic and rounded, good for its own sake rather than a cure for a problem. An excellent example would be the retailer Boots, which has adopted the word 'well-being' in their website address and other communications.

Love

We all need love, in big ways and in small ways. This need is all about social contact, whether one to one or one to many. Any brand involved in bringing people together is tapping this need. You will immediately think of telecommunications companies, brand names such as One 2 One (now absorbed into T-Mobile) and slogans such as BT's 'It's good to talk'. Whichever brand you think of, you can see they are promoting themselves as connecting people. What is evident here is that brands are focusing on the relevant human need, rather than the technology, which is the means to the end.

Notice also how a telephone banking brand such as First Direct has appreciated the pitfalls as well as the benefits of their type of service. It has all the advantages of convenience and practicality in the modern world, but runs the risk of seeming impersonal and losing its human touch. Hence we see adverts stressing their human side, by illustrating their awareness of how robots would make mistakes if they tried to provide a service to human beings.

Closeness

This is about nurturing and being nurtured, and feeling you belong. This means it's connected to family and setting up home, and so it is an important focus for any brand supporting home and family life. This makes it the core need for a category such as pet foods, where the key question for any brand is how to tap into the relationship between the owner and the pet. There is scope for a brand to express this in many ways: think of the independent friend of Kitekat, the cheeky rascal of Felix, or the intimate lover of Sheba. These each overlay a connection to other types of needs, but with an underlying reference to the close emotional tie which is the price of entry to the category.

You will find a wealth of home-oriented activities and brands that look towards this need for closeness, such as gardening or home décor. All of them refer to creating your own little world, somewhere safe and controlled. This is also fruitful territory for any brand tapping into nostalgia. Think Werther's Original toffees, or indeed think of the 'original recipe' variant within the ranges of many food products.

There are magazines and television programmes that connect with all the fundamental needs, but they seem particularly prevalent here. Witness the huge number of TV programmes portraying period dramas or cosy village life, plus the wave of programmes reminding us about 'life as it was in that decade/the best loved/the top 10 of all time' and so on.

Stability

Where the need for Closeness has a lot to say about emotional security and control, the need for Stability is something like an equivalent in the physical world. It has the sense of something sensible, tried and tested, with a good track record and a known history. It knows what it stands for and where it has come from. It is reliable in a wholesome, earthy way, which is connected to (but distinct from) the organisational sense of reliability that is found with the Structure need. It means knowing where you have come from and where you are going. It is Coca-Cola as it has always been – no recipe changes, thank you.

The globalisation trend in the modern world carries with it a loss of roots and local feeling, a potential unsettling of this very need for stability. Hence, many brands need to work on their identity, authenticity, sense of origin and place to become trusted. This is the growth of the need for your brand to tell a coherent story and display a clear provenance. It is real food, grown in what is perceived to be 'the right way'.

Brands with names and marketing emphasising location and history are also tapping the need for Stability, and connecting it with the neighbouring needs of Closeness and Structure. Examples are Yorkshire tea and London Pride beer.

Other Themes

Now we have finished the list, you may be thinking of some themes that appear not to have been covered. The most commonly cited example of this is the desire for sensual pleasure, which is a focus for many brands. The key here is to ask why we want that sensual pleasure in each case. There are many possible needs behind it, and so we find 'pleasure' appearing all over the map. If it's essentially sexual or exciting (e.g. Haagen-Dazs) then it sits in the upper left of the map, but if it's more about feeling cosy and secure (Radox bubble bath) then it may correspond more with the lower right of the map. If it's more about being pampered with luxury so you feel important, then it is more to the left or lower left on the map, while if it's about escape from a routine then it sits somewhere at the top of the map.

2

Further Insight into Needs from Other Perspectives

Different Dimensions

The Number of Needs and Dimensions

Our universal map starts with three major dimensions, and hence six needs, one at each end of each dimension. We then added a further six needs between the others to make a total of 12. However, many maps of this sort in use in market research start with a division using two axes, top to bottom and left to right on the page, so they have four main themes instead of six.

This four-way split is encouraged by the use of computer mapping programs. These take data from a quantitative study and identify a primary dimension (principal component), then a second, a third and so on, but typically print the data on the page with reference to the first two dimensions. The mathematical technique asserts that the dimensions are 'independent' in meaning, implying a logic in showing them at right angles in the map. It also seems simply natural to draw the picture with two dimensions, since you can take any two aspects and cross them in this way.

The two-dimensional approach produces a vertical axis overlapping with *Liberty–Structure* like that on the universal map, and a horizontal axis equivalent to *Self-expression–Love* (see Figure 2.1).

Taking the four poles more widely, it would be more accurate to describe them as four broad concepts:

- 'ideas' (top): curiosity/liberty/ideals;
- 'groundedness' (bottom): practicality/structure/stability;
- 'energy' (left): excitement/self-expression/challenge;
- 'feelings' (right): harmony/love/closeness.

These have been largely covered in the previous commentary for the 12 needs, but we will add a few comments here. The horizontal axis of *energy–feelings* is frequently identified as a *masculine–feminine* or *assertive–affiliative* polarity, describing the personality traits more than the needs or principles. Similarly the vertical axis of *ideas–groundedness* is also described in terms of being open or closed to new things.

When the opposites are reconciled, we get art and science. The creative artist manages to combine the ends of the horizontal axis, by being receptive to impressions and at the same time passionate in expression. On the vertical axis a scientific brand is highly progressive through inventions, but at the same time able to make these very practical and reliable.

These four poles are better interpreted as very broad themes, rather than specific needs. And so, you commonly find the intermediate points added in, to create a system of eight needs. These intermediate needs therefore sit

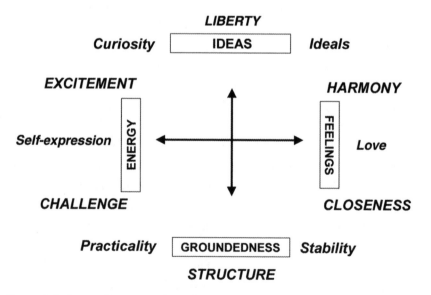

Figure 2.1 A two-dimensional needs map

at the ends of two axes: one top-left to bottom-right, and the other top-right to bottom-left. The first of these contrasts the combination of excitement and curiosity, which you might label 'exploration', with closeness and stability, which you might label 'trust' or 'sincerity'. Trust has been asserted by some commentators as the key to developing a strong brand. Certainly there are some aspects to the word which are fundamental, such as not getting any *nasty* surprises. It does have the capacity to undo everything else, if trust is badly breached, but then so does 'practicality', if the product or service is unreliable. It doubtless has a connection with long-established brands, whose personalities tend to sit lower-right on the map, but this doesn't make it the key driver. It is probably more often a negative driver, one to avoid undermining, than it is a positive driver or key point of differentiation among competitors.

I imagine the research which has led to trust being held up as the key may have suffered from the classic problem of focusing on only one attitude measure. I'm sure you can correlate perceptions of trust against brand purchasing or sales, but you can do that with many other attitude measures. It means trust is worth putting on the list of important candidates, but it does not demonstrate its priority over other issues. This issue will be explored more fully in the next chapter, when we look at brand equity.

The other dimension contrasts the combination of ideals and harmony, which you could label 'style', versus practicality and challenge, which you could label 'substance'. We have said a lot about this contrast already. A further observation would be how this picks up the two aspects of quality, romantic and classic, described by Robert Pirsig in his book *Zen and the Art of Motorcycle Maintenance*.

The eight needs from this system may each be subdivided to create a total of 16. By this stage you are getting down to details, rather than fundamental needs. When this level is applied to brand personality, we find a close fit with the model produced by Jennifer Aaker, reported in David Aaker's book *Building Strong Brands*. Their system comprises five main themes, with subdivisions into 15 more specific traits. They are:

- Sincerity (down-to-earth, honest, wholesome, cheerful) which sits lower right on the map, around stability–closeness–love.

- Sophistication (charming, upper-class) which sits upper right on the map, around harmony–ideals.
- Excitement (up-to-date, imaginative, spirited, daring) which sits at the top and upper left on the map, around liberty–curiosity–excitement.
- Ruggedness (outdoorsy, tough) which sits on the left side, around self-expression and challenge.
- Competence (successful, intelligent, reliable) which sits lower-left and at the bottom of the map, around practicality and structure.

One Super-dimension

However many needs we write down on the universal map, the way it is displayed is mathematically two-dimensional. This is nice to look at on a sheet of paper, but its validity is worth challenging. Why not one or three dimensions?

This is important. Much as many brand managers would like their markets to be multi-dimensional, we often find that most differences between brands can be explained by one super-dimension. This often happens if the brands are primarily positioned on the basis of general quality and price, or if the consumer has become confused by complex marketing messages that promote benefits that don't relate clearly to deeper needs. You can see this in categories where brands are promoted very strongly on functional features that seem to have been invented to be benefits to the consumer. In reality they will only work if they connect with deeper emotional needs.

If you had to collapse the whole thing into one big super-dimension it would lie roughly upper-left to lower-right, around excitement and curiosity versus closeness and stability. You could describe this as a split between active and passive.

Many major dichotomies are related to this dimension. As well as active–passive, we might add other pairings such as:

- levity–gravity
- spirit–substance
- yang–yin

- light–dark
- future–past
- youth–maturity
- confidence–caution
- type A–type B personality.

In terms of brand personality, you tend to find new, up-and-coming brands at the top-left, and mature, long-established brands at the bottom-right.

The emotional loading in Western culture is noticeable on this dimension, with the implication that the upper-left is in some way more desirable than the lower-right. This is very visible in the models of social values that we will see in later chapters, and can also be seen in the coffee example. Words like ordinary and down-to-earth appear at the lower-right, contrasting with excited and energised at the opposite end. This tendency can result in a very negative view of some of the needs placed towards the bottom right of the map, and an overestimation of the desirability of the upper-left characteristics.

Incorporating Price

There is a wide variation in price in many categories, and it tends to be connected with this primary dimension. High-price brands and big spending sit at the upper-left, while simple, 'no nonsense', almost non-branded products sit at the lower-right. The eating-out and drinking-out markets display this pattern, ranging from the 'big night out' (upper-left) where spending is high, down to the simple, quiet drink or meal in the lower-right. You also see it with brands of car. Brands which focus on high price sectors, such as Porsche and Alfa Romeo, are exciting (upper-left), while brands mainly operating in the lower price sectors, such as Ford or Fiat, are positioned as simple and down-to-earth.

These are extreme markets. They involve wide price ranges and high absolute prices, where a large proportion of the population cannot afford the upper price levels. However, the principle still applies to many other categories, even if it is less marked.

Thus, the needs map can be misleading, if it covers wide price ranges so that the brands are not viable alternatives. Simplicity as a benefit becomes confused with low price. It is a good idea in such cases to separate the market into appropriate price bands, and run the needs/benefit mapping separately for each category. Then you can see more clearly the relative positioning and benefits of some brands. For example, you would be able to pick up the excitement of the Mini within a lower price bracket of the car market.

This answers the question about the third dimension mathematically. It would be price. The fullest picture would therefore show the universal map interlocked with the price dimension. You could picture this as something like the slices of a cylinder, leaning over to one side, as shown in Figure 2.2.

In many cases whole categories are based on a specific need, where it acts as a price of entry, something every brand has to work on. Examples are telecommunications, with the Love need, and pet food, with the Closeness need. This does not mean that a brand cannot be differentiated on this need, since it has the possibility to express it in its own unique way.

However, what you also find is that each brand will aim for other needs, as its own trademark. In the cat food example, you find Sheba aiming for glamour (Ideals) and Kitekat or Felix aiming at Excitement and Curiosity. There is no barrier to a specific brand exploiting any of the needs, regardless of the centre of gravity of its category. Indeed, it may be a very good way to subvert the category's conventions and make an impact.

Positives and Negatives

One risk with a strong emphasis on any particular set of needs or benefits is that it may imply a negative on the opposite characteristic. Here are some of the pitfalls of overdoing the expression of each need, or doing it in a negative or extreme way:

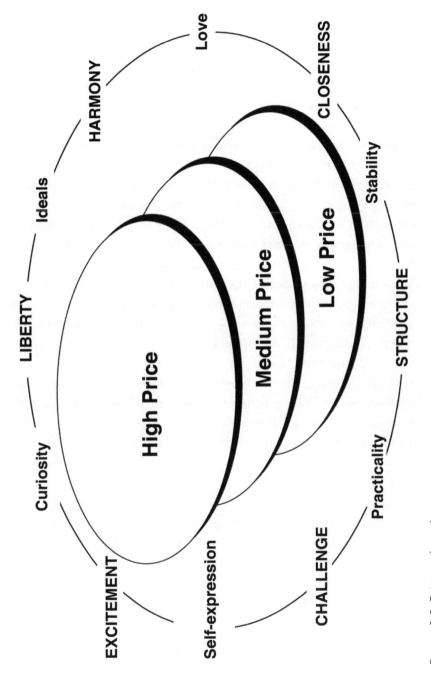

Figure 2.2 Price and needs

- Too much Excitement and not enough Closeness can lead to a lack of trust, a sense that the brand may be too changeable or that it can't be taken seriously. The reverse problem, of too much sincerity and not enough fun, risks seeming too worthy or smothering, somewhat prone to preaching.

- If you overdo the Curiosity need you can overwhelm people with too much information, too many possibilities. Your brand may be seen as changing so fast that it loses any sense of stability and unsettles its customers. They no longer know what they are buying. Conversely, too much stability is boring. Everyone needs a change.

- Too much Liberty and not enough Structure may suggest weirdness, unpredictability, an imitator of others, an obsession with modernity, and perhaps a passing fad. Conversely, too much Structure can mean your brand seems old-fashioned, out of touch, too predictable, bogged down with old ways of thinking and outdated procedures.

- An overemphasis on Ideals risks your brand being seen as impractical, one based on superficial charm, beautiful on the outside. You can also seem elitist and exclusive in a negative way, a risk for a brand such as Sheba. On the other hand, too much Practicality may suggest a lack of style, an overemphasis on clever engineering.

- A strong loading on the Challenge need may imply too much competitiveness. This is a danger for sports drinks brands, which suggest an image of a winner, but don't look as if you should share them with your opponent. Too much Harmony has the reverse problem, a saccharine quality characterised by the overuse of an expression such as 'have a nice day'.

- Too much Love and not enough Self-expression may suggest a brand with a weak personality, something timid and wimpish. Conversely, too much Self-expression can imply aggression, selfishness and a lack of sensitivity or gentleness.

Turning it on its head, some marketing deliberately talks about the avoidance of negative consequences rather than the emphasis of positives. Examples of this would be risk avoidance (for stability) and stupidity avoidance (for practicality).

The Relationship Between Consumers and Brands

The above discussion shows that all the needs are present in every category, and in every price band within a category, even if there is a major set of needs which underpins all brands in that category. So all the needs are relevant and potentially important.

But we can also use the needs map to understand the nature of the *relationship* between people and brands. Here we find some changes in the emphasis through the different ages of branding over the past hundred years.

Figure 2.3 shows three ages of branding, identified with different areas of the universal map, and showing a general evolution in the areas of emphasis.

First Age (Guarantee)

The first age applied broadly to the first half of the twentieth century. The main role of branding was to act as a guarantee that the brand would be an acceptable quality. In those days bad quality could mean *really* bad quality, not just a little lower than you would like it to be. You can identify that age with the lower-right area of the map and the two themes of closeness and structure. It was an age where branding was about the avoidance of negatives – in the one case emotional fears and trust (Closeness) and in the other very down-to-earth considerations of whether the brand was reliable (Structure).

Second Age (Aspiration)

The second age, through the second half of the twentieth century, saw higher quality, and so a reduction in the anxiety side of product judgement, and a growth in brand response that was both outward and upwardly directed. The increased number of brands and the arrival of television advertising brought an increased dimensionality to markets.

It relates to the left side of the map, particularly, as we shall see, when we look later in the book at social values. You could identify the need for Challenge, particularly in the sense of being status-conscious,

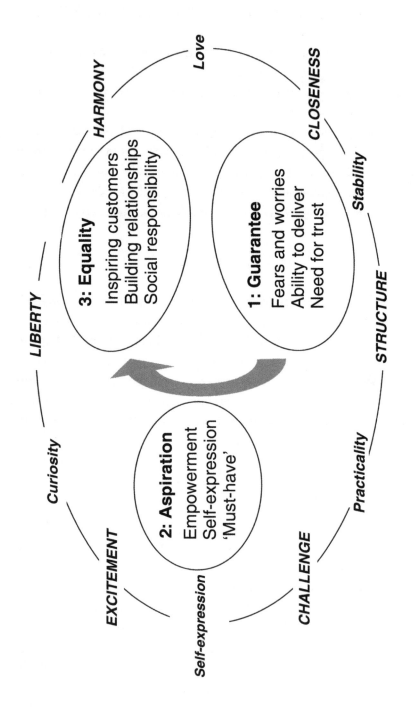

Figure 2.3 The changing relationship

keeping up with the Jones's. You can also see the aspiration and desire relating to the Excitement need. The view of brands as consisting of added values that allowed manufacturers to charge a price premium was a hallmark of this age, and connects with the upper-left of the pricing spectrum.

Third Age (Equality)

Now, as we move into the twenty-first century, we see a number of important changes going on, which connect with an emphasis on the needs of Liberty and Harmony. There is a general change in the structure of branding. International companies are actually in the process of *reducing* the number of brands in their portfolio, mainly as part of a process of internationalisation, although choice is increasing through sub-branding, line extensions and more varieties. Brands are shifting to be defined more by ideas and principles than by benefits specific to one category, which allows them to enter different categories.

For example, the Virgin brand carries a principle of 'cheerful rebellion on behalf of the general public', which can be applied to any category. So we see Virgin trains, planes, financial services, and so on. Where necessary, companies introduce sub-brands under these umbrella brands, and the sub-brand can bring some more specific qualities which drive brand choice within a particular category.

Quality standards are generally higher, leading to more consumer confidence that a brand can enter a category without a track record of performance in that category (again, consider Virgin planes and financial services), or by arranging links that allow them to overcome any barriers. Category boundaries are also breaking down, as new products and services appear that deliberately break the mould.

It means there is now a proliferation of choice, in terms of the quantity and type of brand people can choose to meet their needs, and a culture which is emphasising individuals making their own choices, rather than collective aspirations in the same direction. This obviously connects with an emphasis on the need for Liberty.

At the same time there is a general shift towards the Harmony area of the map, more balanced between internals and externals, with people looking more for principles. You can see something in the consumer demand for more subtlety and real meaning, and you might even recognise some of the anti-branding movement as an expression of these principles. Discussions of branding are moving away from the added values and price premium concepts towards something more holistic. One benefit of having a strong brand may be the ability to charge a premium for it, but many other benefits are recognised as well.

One potential misunderstanding to be avoided is the apparent implication that an ideal modern brand would be positioned on needs in the upper right of the map. This is not the case. We are talking here about the way the brand relates to consumers, not its positioning in terms of the needs it taps into. There are fine examples of brands, such as Nike, who are positioned against needs in the lower left of the map, but which relate to consumers through modern principles.

Building a Relationship with Customers

So, there has been an evolution in the the meaning of a brand to consumers, starting at the lower right and moving upwards through the map to somewhere around the Liberty–Harmony area. This reflects an increase in attempts by modern brands to build relationships with consumers, in principle relationships of equals, rather than the brand on a pedestal talking down to the consumer.

Figure 2.4 describes different aspects of this relationship as it relates to the universal needs map. It is split into three levels: transactions, business principles and connections.

The lowest level is transactions, and this is the least close and personal of the levels. It emphasises impersonal aspects of delivering a product or service to a customer, indeed to any customer. On the one hand it covers consistently and simply delivering the basics. This includes convenience and the avoidance of mistakes or problems. On the other hand it is about

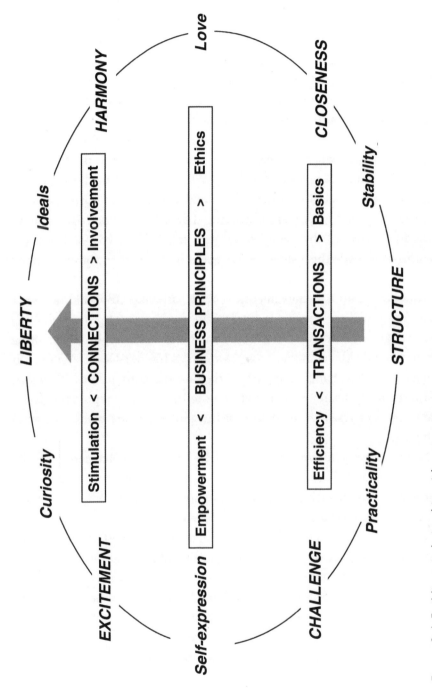

Figure 2.4 Building a relationship with customers

efficiency, including provision of information, product or service performance, and speed of delivery and response to customer enquiries.

On the middle level we have business principles. Relating to the right-hand side of the map, this means the ethics of doing business, incorporating trust, fairness and caring for customers. On the opposite side, we have empowerment, which includes making the customer feel in charge, able to assert themselves and to make individual choices.

The top level of the chart is about the connections between the brand and the customer, where the customer starts to feel close to the brand and to feel the brand is relating very personally to them. On the upper left side we have stimulation, where the brand engages your curiosity, feeds you new ideas and gives you excitement. Towards the upper right side we have involvement, the more emotional side where you feel a close identification with the values of the brand and feel that you are part of something special.

The bottom-to-top movement, towards attempts to build a closer relationship with customers, is reflected in the change of some marketing language and philosophies. In the past, there was a philosophy of marketing labelled 'AIDA', standing for Awareness-Interest-Desire-Action. It emphasised a mechanistic approach, treating the consumer as an object, first to be made aware of the brand, then to have their interest stimulated, and so on. Key research indicators for this philosophy are brand awareness and trial.

More modern philosophies are based on building involvement with the brand. As we shall see in Chapter 3 on brand equity, they emphasise research indicators such as 'depth of familiarity or understanding the brand' as opposed to 'simple awareness of the brand'.

There is some danger that this shift appears to suggest that the lower levels of the map are no longer important. But a brand's attempts to build a relationship will be undermined if you can't get the basics of delivery right. Think of American Express, who work hard to emphasise the involvement aspect of connecting with their customers, but have the problem that many restaurants, hotels and retailers in the UK refuse to accept the card, even if they have a sign in the window suggesting they do. The brand is undermined by the basics.

It is a matter of some debate how much customers of some types of service actually want to have a relationship with a service provider. When people say they don't want a relationship, what they probably mean is they want a certain sort of relationship, where the company is not too intrusive, or they feel there are immediate service delivery issues to be addressed. A company which can get service delivery right, and adapt their way of communicating to the temperament or preferences of their customers, will be able to do a good job of building a relationship.

Establishing a close relationship between the customer and the brand has consequences for how the brand handles changes. Coca-Cola and Marks & Spencer are two long-established brands which have become closely entwined with the lives of many of their customers. Those people felt alienated when each of these brands introduced certain changes, in the one instance the new product formulation for Coke, and in the other a new line of fashion which didn't suit the core customers of Marks & Spencer. With hindsight, these were both marketing mistakes, but the point is that the relationship can grow so close that customers feel they 'own' the brand, which can make it difficult for the brand to introduce new ideas.

Other Psychological Systems

The general structure of the universal map appears in diverse places, including those whose origin is not in the analysis of brands. Indeed, the shape of the map does seem to be embedded in the structure of human life and psychology, and this should provide some feeling of confidence that the framework has the consistency and the depth we have claimed it has. Let's now look at a few of these systems, in order to demonstrate this point.

The principle underpinning most of the systems discussed below is an attempt to classify people into different types. We will return to this approach in the chapter on 'segmentation', discussing its merit as a marketing tool. Here we want to establish that the framework is consistent with the universal map, and to see how some of the thinking behind these systems has influenced our thinking about consumers' needs.

Maslow's Hierarchy of Needs

This is probably the most familiar modern system concerning human needs. It was developed by an American psychologist, Maslow, in the 1950s. Since then its format has evolved slightly and many companies claim to have used it in developing typology systems. In practice these systems work with people's claimed motivations and drives, rather than with their deeper needs, of which they may not be aware. It is therefore best to focus solely on Maslow's system rather than any others it appears to have inspired.

Figure 2.5 shows the conventional representation of the hierarchy as a pyramid, alongside a reworking of it according to the universal map. The original system had five levels of needs: physiological, safety, love/belonging, esteem and self-actualisation. Cognition and aesthetics were added at a later stage.

A core concept was that the lower level needs have to be reasonably well satisfied, before you become concerned with the higher needs. For example, the need for food and shelter (physiological) would take precedence over any interest in love and belonging or esteem. On a very fundamental level, this seems reasonable, but not particularly useful to marketers. It means, for practical purposes in most developed countries, that the action zone for brand positioning in the original system covered only esteem and love or belonging. Self-actualisation was pretty much above everything mundane, while concern with the safety or physiology needs operated at the basic level of food and shelter.

Reading Maslow's original book on the subject, he never intended the physiology or safety needs to include positive aspects of physical expression. He would have viewed activities such as baking a cake or fixing a bicycle as *drives*, capable of fulfilling any of the needs according to your reason for doing these things. You can bake a cake to please someone (love) or to win praise or feel good about yourself (esteem).

Even allowing for this clarification, there is still a difficulty with the hierarchical construction. It conflicts with the finding that people with very limited resources will blow a large sum on a television set, rather than get more food. Similarly, all sorts of people are into self-improvement and further education outside school or university, not just those with high resources.

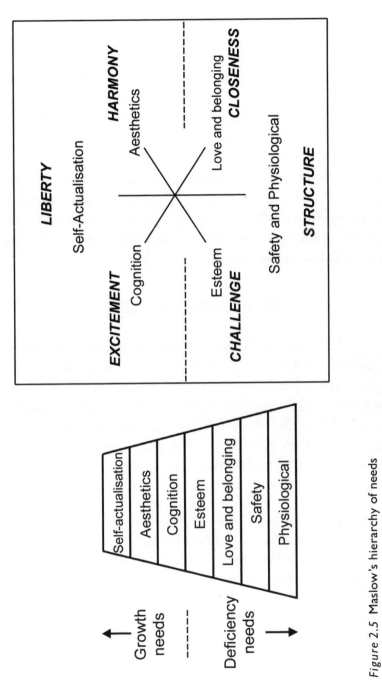

Figure 2.5 Maslow's hierarchy of needs

Setting aside those issues, we can connect Maslow's needs with the big six on the universal map. Taking the seven-level version of Maslow's pyramid, we could identify physiological and safety with Structure, love and belonging with Closeness, and esteem with Challenge. Further up, cognition would go with Excitement, aesthetics with Harmony and self-actualisation with Liberty. Some of Maslow's levels were identified as deficiency needs, and they all appear below half-way on the universal map. The remainder were considered growth needs, and they appear above half-way.

Alternatively, you might feel it fits better if you start with the older system of five levels and place them top, bottom, right and left: combine physiology and safety at the bottom, love and belonging on the right, esteem on the left and self-actualisation at the top. You might reasonably add the two newer ones in as offshoots, connecting them with curiosity (cognition) and ideals (aesthetics).

Jung's Personality Typology

Now we turn attention to theories in modern psychology. Notable among these, and widely referenced by market researchers, are the theories of C.G. Jung, illustrated in Figure 2.6.

Jung identified four 'functions': thinking, feeling, sensation and intuition. He also talked about these in terms of types of people, e.g. a thinking type or a feeling type, but I am more interested in these concepts as principles of expression or need, than in classifying types of people. The four functions are closely identified with the up, down, left and right sides of the universal map:

- Curiosity/Liberty/Ideals – Thinking function;
- Harmony/Love/Closeness – Feeling function;
- Stability/Structure/Practicality – Sensation function;
- Challenge/Self-expression/Excitement – Intuition function.

These functions were considered to have varying compatibility with each other. In particular, Jung asserted that thinking was incompatible with feeling and sensation incompatible with intuition. This would lead you to expect thinking to appear opposite feeling on the map, and intuition

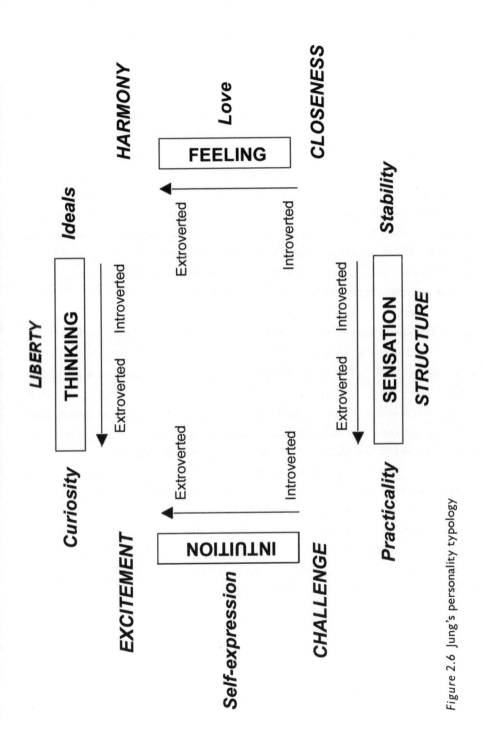

Figure 2.6 Jung's personality typology

opposite sensation, but this is not the case. Incompatible or not, these functions do appear in the neighbouring places when we empirically generate maps of needs, whether or not they are considered to mix in the human personality.

Jung also placed a strong emphasis on distinguishing extroversion and introversion, splitting each of the functions into an extroverted and an introverted form. Rather than insisting on an 'either or' split, I think it's useful to view it as a spectrum for each of the functions. This is suggested by the arrows shown in the figure. So, thinking ranges from an extroverted form in Curiosity through to a more introverted form in Ideals. Feeling may be considered relatively more extroverted in its expression of Harmony, and more introverted in Closeness. Sensation is practical when extroverted, and concerned with a sense of stability when introverted. Intuition is more extroverted when looking for Excitement, and more introverted when considering a sense of Challenge.

These links may be felt to be weak. After all, many of the needs seem to have an introverted and an extroverted expression. This is particularly true of those in the upper right and lower left parts of the map, around Ideals/Harmony and Challenge/Practicality. The broader theme is that extroversion is more associated with the upper left, and introversion with the lower right. But this needs care, since there are at least two or three distinct meanings of the words extroverted and introverted.

In one case they mean personality traits – open, friendly and talkative (extroverted) versus closed, private and uncommunicative (introverted). This version lies roughly top and bottom on the map. In another sense they are about social values – concerned with the outer world and material expression (extroverted) versus the inner world and private impressions (introverted). This places them more on a left to right axis. Jung's version is somewhere between the two, so extroversion appears upper left and introversion lower right.

Personality Mapping

There are various systems for classifying or mapping personality, some looking at human traits, others based empirically on brands. Some systems used in market research use human personality or psychology as a basis for brand personality, with the assumption that any human trait can be projected onto brands.

Figure 2.7 shows the general framework of such maps. The vertical and horizontal axes shown in the centre of the figure refer to the labels found in the Social Styles system, as used by Wilson Learning. This is a system which has been applied in the business world, across a great many professions and industries. It interprets the vertical axis in terms of an orientation to people (top end) or tasks (bottom end). The horizontal axis presents alternative ways of dealing with people, either 'I tell' or 'I ask'. These are slightly more specific terms for what is often identified as extrovert-introvert (vertical axis) and assertive or affiliative (horizontal axis). In terms of brand personality traits, the vertical axis is typically labelled progressive and inventive versus traditional and reliable. The horizontal axis is dynamic and forceful versus accessible and friendly. These systems are visibly very close and connected to the universal needs map.

Social Values

Various systems exist based on human values, what you believe in or what matters to you, rather than your personality. There are variations between them, but the general pattern is illustrated in Figure 2.8.

This has some overlap with the personality mapping, although it is theoretically distinct. It is feasible for someone to have conservative social values, but at the same time to have an upbeat personality and be very open and interested in meeting different people. Equally you can find people who are very concerned with achievement and material success, but have quiet, gentle personalities. Having said that, it is more likely that someone who is very open and curious will have more progressive social values, and that someone with strong worldly ambitions will display an assertive personality in their pursuit of those desires.

From our point of view, the shape is fundamentally similar when we connect it to the universal map, even if they are taking slices through the

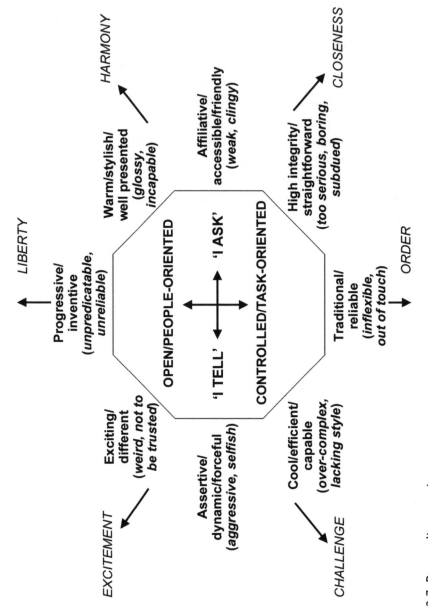

Figure 2.7 Personality mapping

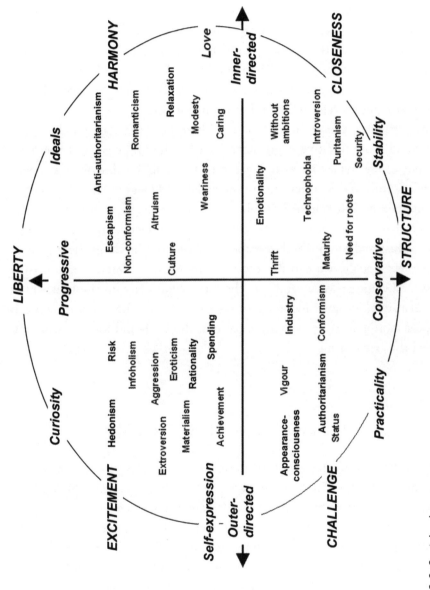

Figure 2.8 Social values

subject at slightly different angles. The social values version shows strong connections with the universal map. It highlights beliefs or behaviour which are likely to be found as someone pursues each need: for example, the values of 'risk-taking' and 'infoholic' connect with curiosity, while 'puritanism' and 'security concerns' connect with stability.

Another aspect that comes through in most social value maps is a judgemental tendency about different areas of the map. I have tried to include both positive and negative phrases in all areas of the map, though this is not always reflected by other commentators.

In particular, you often find more positive language used for the upper parts and more negative expressions used for the lower parts of the map. People whose values lie near the top of the map are described as open-minded, enthusiastic, interested in the wider world and the development of themselves as fully rounded people. By contrast, people with values in the lower areas of the map may be called narrow-minded, stick-in-the-mud, isolationist and so on. Doubtless there are people who do fit these general types, but equally we can flip the positive–negative descriptions in each case. The progressive end of the spectrum can manifest itself as irresponsible, escapist, inconsistent and unrealistic. The opposite end can appear more positively as mature, patient, thorough and loyal to what has stood the test of time.

The Hereford Mappa Mundi (World Map)

All the systems we have just examined are frameworks for understanding human psychology. The last one I want to look at is something different – a historical document that I think reveals something about the psychology or world view of its designers, which connects with the universal needs map. This is unlikely to give you much insight into how to market a brand today, but I hope it illustrates the principles at work, even if you feel the connection with the universal map is a matter of personal judgement.

Figure 2.9 shows a simplified version of the medieval Hereford Mappa Mundi, or world map. The real thing can be viewed in Hereford Cathedral.

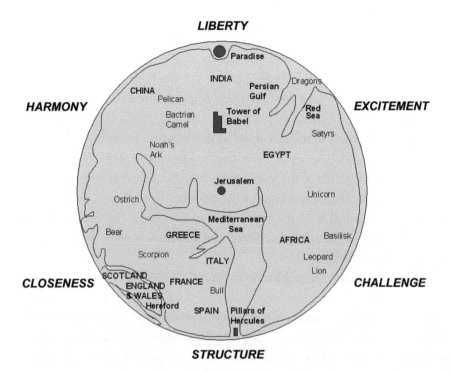

Figure 2.9 The Hereford Mappa Mundi
Inspired by the Mappa Mundi, with thanks to Hereford Cathedral.

I have picked out a small number of details from what is a much larger, more complex set of information in the original. The positions of each place name, creature and the shape of the map are faithful to the real map, but I have been selective in what I have highlighted. The actual map is about a metre in diameter, incorporating illustrations and text with abundant detail. It also has a large border, which I have not shown, with extra information, illustrations and comment.

The Hereford map is the best surviving example of a medieval world map, created between the twelfth and fourteenth centuries. These maps were variations on the same ideas, heavily copied from each other, and believed to originate in Roman times. Their purpose was nearer to religious education than precise cartography. Relative positions of key places are broadly correct in most cases, but the sizes and shapes of large areas are heavily distorted. They were more concerned to show ideas and items of interest than how to travel somewhere. The places and creatures shown are frequently mythological or symbolic. The general shape is referred to as a T-O design, meaning the map was drawn in a circle (an O) with the main continents divided by a T shape. Europe is in the bottom left, Africa in the bottom right and Asia in the upper half of the picture. Hence, east is at the top, west at the bottom, north to the left and south to the right. This covered the known, inhabited world at that time (as far as the English were concerned). Jerusalem is placed in the middle of the map.

Around the outside of the map I have added the six major needs from the universal map. The orientation of the map has been flipped over from left to right, so you will see harmony and closeness on the left, and excitement and challenge on the right. Liberty and structure remain at the top and bottom respectively.

At the top of the Hereford map we find Paradise. The details on the map show Adam and Eve being expelled from the Garden of Eden, and in the border at the top is a picture of Christ. At the bottom are the Pillars of Hercules, symbols of structural support. This therefore fits well with the axis of liberty–structure, but is presented in a very judgemental way. Up is good and godly, down is earthly.

The British Isles and North-Western Europe are the homeland, sitting next to the need for closeness. Creatures shown in this area of the map include a bear, known for its ferocious protection of its offspring. Further up on the left-hand side in the region associated with harmony, we find Noah's Ark, China and the pelican. The Ark symbolises caring for others, the animals two-by-two, while the pelican is an idealistic creature, feeding its young with the blood from its own chest. On the other side, next to challenge we find the basilisk, leopard and lion. Anyone familiar with *Harry Potter and The Chamber of Secrets* will know the basilisk to be a very challenging creature. In the area of excitement we find satyrs and dragons. You will also note the position of Jerusalem as a spiritual centre, and above it the Tower of Babel, aspiring to Paradise. God's punishment for building the tower emphasises that the top of the map is good and heavenly.

My contention is that the overall shape of the Hereford map is therefore connected with the universal needs map, at least in the broad themes. Care should be taken over the detail, but I think the big patterns are the same.

Conclusions and Implications for Brands

Having presented all these systems, let's try to draw some conclusions and implications for brand management:

- The general structure arises everywhere, in many guises and contexts, but still with the same shape. This suggests that this framework is fundamental and reliable. You can change the precise words used for the labels, and use different numbers of them if you wish, but the underlying meaning is consistent.

- The various pictures we have shown have highlighted different ways of connecting with people, which is the basis for brand success. You could draw on any of these, and many others, as inspiration for how to do this, variations on the ways of showing connections between your brand and people's needs.

- The biggest danger, and a pitfall even today, seems to be the risk of judging one set of needs to be higher and more worthy than others. The needs at the bottom of the map are equally valid and powerful as those towards the top of the map. We will see in Chapter 7 how this perspective is increasingly important for understanding the potential for brands.

3

Brand Equity: How do People Assess your Brand Overall?

This chapter discusses brand equity, a topic much argued over and poorly understood. Over the past decade we have probably witnessed the classic path: an initial high surge of interest, then a period of some disillusionment, and now a more stable development of brand management incorporating brand equity as an important tool.

There remains some confusion, since the term 'brand equity' is used in some contexts to signify the financial value of a brand as an asset on a firm's balance sheet, but in market research circles it is now generally taken to mean the strength of a brand based on consumer appeal. There has also been much debate about whether brand equity should be taken to mean the detail of people's strong associations with a brand, but on the whole it is now primarily a summary of the main components of brand strength. Researchers will continue to argue over how to measure it, but they tend to agree on its main purpose for the brand manager: to indicate the underlying strength of consumer desire for the brand, when you strip away factors such as strength of distribution and marketing support.

When we looked at brand positioning in Chapters 1 and 2, we explored how brands focus on particular human needs and more specific attributes relevant to the product or service category in which the brand operates. The question that follows is, 'How well has the brand done the job – how much do people want that brand?' Is it simply one big summary measure, or are there a number of strands to this question? The answer is both yes and no. We can summarise it into one overall score, but we can also usefully identify a number of strands within it that constitute building blocks for all brands.

The Concept of Summary Evaluations

I would define brand equity as:

- in total, the desire for a brand based on all its attitudes; and
- summarised by a small number of building blocks or summary evaluations.

These summary evaluations are broad concepts which are applicable across all categories. They are measures of attitudes towards brands, not measures of consumer behaviour. One example is 'differentiation'. This means the extent to which the brand is offering something different from other competing brands. Another example is 'familiarity', meaning how well the brand is known and understood by people.

They take the 'pie' that is the associations that people have with brands, and slice it a different way from the analysis of needs. Summary evaluations are the end result, whereas the brand positioning described by the needs represents the means to that end. Two brands may be positioned very differently, but overall they may have achieved the same level of differentiation, familiarity and so on.

The perceptions and needs underpin and explain the summary evaluations. Your brand may be relevant (summary evaluation) because it is strong, full-bodied, and so on. It may be different because it is more exotic than other brands. The summary evaluations give you the overall audit, and the perceptions tell you why, and give you ideas about what you might change if you wished to.

It is a matter of debate whether you wish to say that the detailed perceptions *drive* the summary evaluations, which in turn sum to create a total equity. This certainly sounds rather too mechanistic as a description of the mind of an individual human being, as they assess whether they want a brand. It does, however, seem reasonable to suggest that each person makes some kind of shorthand evaluation of brands, consciously or unconsciously, and that this is probably along the lines of the summary evaluations. For example, they may sum up, 'This brand is better quality than the others, but it lacks some features I need so it's not relevant to me'. Or, more likely, they do a much less coherent, conscious version of this.

Whatever the case, it is valuable to look at summary measures that we can compare across categories, so that we can learn from different brands in different situations. The important challenge is to identify these big attitudinal building blocks, which we aim to do below.

Work on Attitudes, not Behaviour

But first, why all this focus on attitudes? Do attitudes drive behaviour, or does behaviour drive attitudes? The answer is yes to both.

We can see that behaviour drives attitudes, as follows. Users of a brand nearly always have higher opinions of it than non-users of a brand. This is partly what you would expect, assuming people have been free to choose whether or not to use the brand. But it also happens because usage reinforces our attitudes. Given that all our judgements are subjective, the more we use a brand the more we feel confident about it, generally speaking. We become more familiar with it, we are able to appreciate some of its qualities that may not be apparent to non-users of the brand, and we see the many little ways in which it differs from other brands. Furthermore, we feel connected to that brand and therefore more likely to speak up for it, not least to avoid the risk of looking stupid – who wants to say they choose to buy a brand that lets them down so badly in many ways?

So behaviour does drive attitudes, but this cannot be the whole picture. If that were the case on its own, then marketing strategies based purely on pushing the brand towards the consumer would dominate. Marketing would consist of acts encouraging or even forcing the consumer to try a product, in the knowledge that this would trigger a positive attitude, which should then lead to more usage, and so on. But very obviously, users of a brand do in many cases form a negative view of the brand, making them desire to switch brands. Switching is not totally explained by this, but it is certainly a big reason.

The reasonable view is therefore that there is a reinforcing circle of attitudes and behaviour, both driving each other to some extent. Most importantly, research has shown a connection between a brand's future success and the balance between its consumer attitudes and its purchasing. Where attitudes are weaker than purchasing, it tends to anticipate decline. Where attitudes are currently stronger than purchasing, we tend to find future growth. This is the general pattern, though some care is needed with brands that are very long-established or market-leading. Here we sometimes find that purchase loyalty drops, while attitudes remain very positive, resulting from a general shift in consumer behaviour towards wider repertoires – they still believe the leading brand is the best, but they now use a greater variety of brands for different occasions.

This general priority of attitudes over behaviour also shows why many price promotions driving short-term behavioural loyalty, or the attraction of some new buyers, fail to drive future success. It will only work if the behaviour is backed up and surpassed by a change in attitudes to the brand. Otherwise, the brand tends to be in a worse position after the promotion is withdrawn than it was before the promotion took place. There are, of course, good reasons to use promotions tactically, such as getting rid of products that will soon pass a 'best before' date, making way for a new improved version, or stimulating the trial of a completely new product where high price might be a barrier to trial. But generally, price promotions on established brands fail to attract many new buyers and tend to encourage shopping behaviour based on price hunting.

The lesson is that a brand manager should give priority to working on attitudes, not on behaviour. This may in some cases require stimulating a trial first, in order that people develop awareness of a benefit that can only be discovered from using the brand. Or it may mean a broader approach to marketing, with the intention of encouraging an attitude to the brand among everyone, buyers and non-buyers alike. In the first case behaviour will broadly precede attitudes, while in the second case the reverse will apply. Either way, the company is building the brand through working on attitudes, not behaviour.

Identifying Candidates for Brand Equity Building Blocks

When companies talk about having a model of brand health or brand equity, it is typically 'big attitudinal building blocks' that they are dealing with. These may sometimes include behavioural measures, although we recommend essentially focusing on attitudes for the reasons given above.

To qualify as building blocks, they must carry some sort of reason for wanting the brand. Otherwise they are just 'global attitudes', roughly equivalent to equity as a whole. For example, phrases such as 'a brand I prefer', 'my favourite brand', 'the best brand for me' all express a global attitude since there is no 'reason why' contained within them. Marketing cannot act on them, it can only make them move as a consequence of doing something more specific.

Considering specific building blocks, you might think there were endless numbers of them that could contribute to the desire for the brand, and that these would vary across categories. In fact, a small number of consistent themes emerge. Sometimes you find the opposite view, a reductionist perspective promoting one thing only as the key to brand equity. I have seen many articles and books taking this stance, singling out either brand trust, quality or top-of-mind brand awareness. I'm sure there are others. This trap arises through some problematical characteristics of research data: the reinforcement of attitudes by behaviour, the brand halo effect, and accidental correlation. The first of these has just been explained, the other two are explained below.

Brand Halo Effect

People tend to make a global judgement about a brand, consciously or unconsciously. When you ask them questions about a brand they are very close to, they tend to give positive answers to *all* the questions, with some slight adjustments around a generally high score. For example, if they are asked to give marks out of 10 to the brand for many different aspects, on average they might give a score of 9, with the individual answers to each question ranging between 8 and 10. Conversely, a person who is very distant from the brand may give scores scattered between 3 and 7, with an average score of 5.

This happens for two reasons. First, there is a knock-on effect between the issues covered by the questions. As an illustration, consider a queue at a supermarket checkout. If the queue is short, then a customer will feel happier, and this will make them feel that the member of staff on the till is more friendly. However, if the queue is long, the customer becomes annoyed and they tend to judge the member of staff more harshly, regardless of how well that person tries to please the customer. The consequence is that judgements of queue length and staff friendliness may be very similar.

A second reason is that many perceptions people express are actually 'acts of faith' rather than careful evaluations. For example, researching pet foods many years ago it was well known that the leading brand, Whiskas, had a relatively poor smell. But in research studies the ratings for Whiskas on the dimension of smell were more positive than for other brands.

The net result of all this is that strong brands score highly on everything, which we call the brand halo effect, and some of these scores are a consequence of people's global liking for the brand, rather than true evaluations.

Accidental Correlation

We are all prone to making assumptions about cause and effect, when we see apparent connections between things. Often we may be right, but there is always a danger of picking on something that is an irrelevant, accidental characteristic, or does not operate in the way we think.

As an example, suppose you observed in your neighbourhood an increase in the number of police, and at the same time an increase in the frequency of buses. You believe there is a connection, but you might make mistakes in trying to explain cause and effect. Perhaps the police are there to safeguard the buses (i.e. 'more buses causes more police'), or the buses are there to provide transport for the police (i.e. 'more police causes more buses'), or both events may be a result of a change of local government policy (i.e. 'police and buses are caused by a third factor, they do not influence each other').

I have picked this somewhat unusual example, because it shows that *any* of these three explanations is possible. You simply cannot tell at first sight which is true. Often there will be some other information that will help you decide, but this is not always the case. So here is the warning: be very careful about your assumptions of cause and effect, since you may well be wrong.

A Combination of Difficulties

When you put the above difficulties together (the reinforcement of attitudes by behaviour, the brand halo effect, and accidental correlation), we hit a big problem: almost *any* brand attitude measure will show a good correlation with any brand behaviour measure, including sales. The connection will always appear strong mathematically, and it will look as though the attitude is driving (causing) the sales.

And it means you immediately run into two problems if you focus your investigations on just one attitude measure:

- *Accidental effect*: The correlation you see against sales may be accidental, as in the police and buses example. It will look persuasive, but it could be misleading. The key may be a third factor that you haven't included in your research.
- *Missing the complete picture*: If you only study one attitude, you will stand no chance of deducing its importance as a driver of brand success. You have to include at least the majority of other good candidates, and then with more sophisticated data analysis you can measure the differences in their contribution.

This is bad news for any big piece of investigation which has only looked at one attitude dimension and established a correlation with sales. The second issue means you have no idea how it contributes alongside other issues, and the first issue means you can't even be sure whether the fit is real or accidental, without some other supporting evidence.

The first problem (accidental effect) is probably *not* the major issue for the three dimensions I picked out above (trust, quality and top-of-mind brand awareness). But, I do think 'trust' can be a bit close to a global attitude, meaning all you are saying is, 'They like this brand or they want this brand'. It's what you do to build trust or to break trust that is more interesting. And I believe the problem with top-of-mind brand awareness is that it rises *and falls* directly according to marketing activity. It is not a sustained input to brand strength. Quality, on the other hand, is definitely a good candidate for the list.

A bigger problem is the need to have as many candidates as possible in the list, to get close to the complete picture. So, to be honest, I tend to ignore any report that has looked at only one or two attitude dimensions, no matter how well executed the piece of work.

I have seen various 'serious' pieces of investigative research in this area. To qualify for that title in my mind, the model arising from the research must have worked back from some measure of consumer behaviour or in-market performance, and tried to explain it in terms of attitudes. In every one of these cases they identify at least four or five dimensions as a minimum that are necessary, allowing for the possibility of some more that may be relevant to certain categories or specific brands.

If you look at the spirit and attempt to observe the concepts at work in these models, underneath the different ways of measuring things and glueing them together as reported outputs, you find more commonality than difference. Or put another way, I think there are some genuinely recurring important concepts whose existence is easily explained, even if there are large variations in the way different research agencies or consultants might measure them or use them in their models. Obviously the way things are measured, analysed and reported is crucial in their usefulness to a brand manager, but here I am concerned far more with the understanding we can gain from identifying the concepts.

Main Attitudinal Building Blocks

Figure 3.1 lists and illustrates the big building blocks I have picked out.

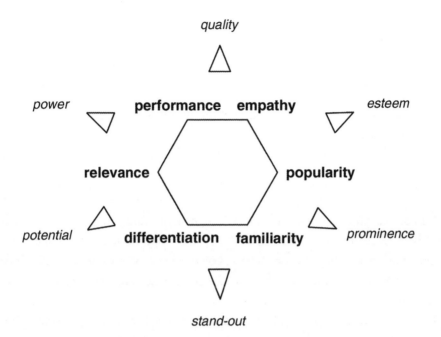

Figure 3.1 Equity building blocks

It shows a hexagon with six components in the middle:

- familiarity
- differentiation
- relevance
- performance
- empathy
- popularity.

These six are reasonably distinct, and all contribute something different to brand success. They do, however, combine in revealing ways, and around the outside of the chart are shown another six themes:

- stand-out
- potential

- power
- quality
- esteem
- prominence.

Let's focus first on the six components attached to the hexagon in the middle of Figure 3.1.

Familiarity

There is a broad dimension that we might call brand awareness, although this is likely to be misleading. At its most shallow it simply means the recognition of a brand name when shown a list of names, as in, 'Which of these brands of instant soup have you seen or heard of?' Technically we call this 'prompted awareness' (or aided awareness).

Slightly more challenging is the ability to recall the name *without* being shown a list, but still prompted by a mention of the category, as in the question, 'What brands of instant soup can you think of?' We call this spontaneous awareness (or unaided awareness). You might wish to focus on the brand mentioned first, which we call 'top-of-mind awareness'.

It sounds straightforward, but increasingly it can run into difficulties in the modern world, as brands cross category boundaries and it becomes harder to define whether something is a brand, a sub-brand or a 'variant' within a brand. The crux is that it is difficult to know *what* exactly someone has recalled. Have they got in their mind what you think they have, when they mention the magic word? It highlights the danger of considering the brand name to be a clear, perfect label for the brand. The name is far from being the only trigger that cues people into identifying a brand. In response to the question, 'Which brand do you use?' some people may mention other branding devices that identify the brand, such as logos, slogans or characters – as in 'I use the one with the rabbit on it'.

This should be no surprise in a world where there are simply so many brands that we stand no chance of remembering all the names, even in some cases when we actually use the product! It is a classic problem in readership research, where it is known as 'title confusion'. Even using prompted lists of names, it has been found helpful to present those names in the typeface as they appear on each publication.

Perhaps partly because of this potential confusion, and the lack of clarity of exactly what it is that someone has recalled, measures such as prompted awareness have been found to play *no* part in brand equity. These awareness measures do go up in response to advertising, and sales may well go up at the same time, but this is a reaction to marketing push. The underlying desire for the brand (equity) may not have gone up, as you would see when the awareness scores decay back to their original level after the advertising finishes.

The awareness concept that *has* been found to be important in brand equity is more about depth of understanding or familiarity with what the brand stands for. It means someone has to claim they know more than just the name of the brand, although it may be unwise to put them on the spot and ask them exactly what they know. Their 'knowledge' may consist of a collection of rather elusive impressions, and not necessarily relate clearly to any explicit property of the brand. If there is a clear hook, then you might conclude that the link is a stable one, but it would be unwise to underestimate the strength of less tangible associations.

There are two aspects within the concept of familiarity, but in practice they work closely together. They are:

- the clarity of what a brand stands for; and
- the strength of communication of what it stands for.

A person tends to be clear about what a brand stands for if its identity has been strongly and consistently communicated, and if one person is clear about it then it is likely that others are similarly clear and hold the same view.

When brands grow, in the early stages we usually see familiarity growing ahead of the other equity components. You need to get up some steam to get started. Put another way, people are unlikely to adopt the brand unless they are clear what it is they are adopting.

In fact, it seems to be the case that you need to generate a reasonable level of familiarity for a brand to get off the ground, but once past that point other factors come into play, in particular relevance and differentiation.

Obviously advertising is one mechanism for getting this familiarity started, but it is not the only one. Indeed, the most powerful force seems to be the general public. If you can get your brand talked about, then you will generate momentum. Look at the example of Tango, where the face-slapping action and slogan 'you know when you've been Tangoed' became part of popular culture, and could be seen being acted out in children's playgrounds.

Differentiation

Differentiation is an obvious component of brand equity. If you fail to offer anything different from your competitors, then there is no reason for consumers to consider switching to your brand. And similarly, if you view brands as if they were 'political candidates for election' to be voted for by the general public, then you can see that two candidates with similar views are going to receive a split vote. The two brands will have to share the votes among those consumers who are interested in that sort of product or service.

Having said that, in some cases the presence of multiple brands offering the same kind of thing can be a benefit to all of them. A branch of a fast-food restaurant often does better if there is a competitor nearby, since the presence of both of them encourages consumers to think of buying fast food. It doesn't help market share, but it does grow the market.

There are two broad approaches to creating differentiation. The traditional route is to perform noticeably above average on important performance dimensions, e.g. the dimension of aroma for coffee. Ideally, the aim is to dominate the attribute or dimension. The more modern route is to find your own unique way of expressing an important attribute or dimension.

The traditional approach also tended to be based on 'added aspiration'. Desirable personality traits could be added on. The more modern view is that the characteristic differences need to be more authentic, more deeply integrated into the brand, and must be consistently presented throughout all the different 'touchpoints' between the consumer and the brand. For example, a brand such as The Gap presents an informality and collective feeling through its adverts, staff, products and in-store environment. Conversely, Abbey (formerly Abbey National bank) ran into difficulties through implying a 'good guys' personality via its advertising, but at the same time imposing service charges for the use of certain competitors' cashpoint machines. The size of the charge was unimportant, in fact it was very small, but the problem lay in the inconsistency of the brand experience. The advertising said one thing while the usage contradicted it.

It may appear from this that branding has gone full circle, starting with authentic quality issues, passing through a phase of image aspiration, and now back towards product-specific features. In fact, the original phase focused on doubts about whether a brand was good enough to do the job, whereas the issue is now about being different in the way you do the job. It can be about product or service features, but it is equally likely to be about something more emotional, less tangible but still very real. It has become a question of each brand being able to 'tell its own story' and to provide customers with a complete experience. To quote Howard Schultz of Starbucks Coffee Company: 'Customers see themselves inside our company . . . part of the Starbucks experience.'

The importance of differentiation is high in most models of brand equity, particularly with regard to the outlook for the future. Differentiation is often the first thing to fall for a large brand that is running into trouble. However, too much differentiation can be a problem. It appears to go hand-in-hand with a niche positioning that limits the brand's suitability to a minority of people or usage occasions, so we tend to find that behavioural loyalty drops for cases of very high differentiation.

Differentiation is also growing in importance as a mechanism for attracting attention in the first place, not just for having something different to say once people have got as far as considering a brand. In a world where most categories are overloaded with choice, and the volume of advertising and brand experiences is constantly spiralling upwards, it is imperative to find new ways of standing out from the crowd. Having something different to say is likely to add to the stand-out of any marketing activity.

Differentiation may be pursued through many different strategies. The motto in advertising is not 'if you can't beat them, join them', but 'if you can't beat them, change the rules of the game'. This kind of disruption strategy means refusing to accept the ways consumers currently judge brands in terms of dimensions and performance. It means making them rethink, and often turning an apparent negative into a positive.

Think of the award-winning Guinness advert with the opening line, 'He waits, that's what he does'. The advert goes on to involve the viewer in an experience of the quality resulting from that waiting. In a world where we generally find increased speed and convenience to be the winning formula, this challenges you to think the opposite. It is going on the attack with a tangible, authentic point of difference: the fact that you wait a long time for a pint of Guinness to be poured.

Further back in time we might point to the Smash adverts, using the 'Martians'. These used the device of suggesting that mashed potato made by traditional means (boiling potatoes then smashing them to pieces) would be a laughably low-quality way of doing things. Again, this was taking a point of difference and turning it into a positive. Of course, there were also other reasons why these adverts were so successful, but they illustrate a point: if you have a strong point of difference, you can turn it to your advantage.

The widely held view is that product differences are becoming harder to generate, as manufacturers or service providers are becoming swifter and more successful at copying each other. This means that emotional benefits are growing in importance over functional benefits, certainly as a point of differentiation between competing brands.

An interesting case is the Vauxhall (Opel) Zafira. This is an MPV (a multi-purpose vehicle), competing with models such as the Citroën Picasso, Renault Scenic, Ford Galaxy and so on. Now the Zafira does have a tangible point of difference; its Flex-7 seating system. There is a third row of seats, which normally lie flat under the boot space. It only takes a couple of minutes to raise those seats into position (it works – I've tried it). The idea is therefore that, from a five-seater vehicle, you have the load space *and* the passenger carrying capacity of a larger, seven-seater MPV, although admittedly not both at the same time.

My memory is that the advertising for the car used to lean heavily on this feature, promoting the cleverness of the designers. I'm sure it conveyed the message successfully about this feature and its technical excellence. However, more recent adverts have changed tack. They now show a father, able to please his kids by giving their friends a ride, with the strap line 'Daddy Cool'. The feature that allows this to happen is still present, but the benefit plays much more heavily on the emotional angle. This would seem to illustrate the movement towards working on emotional benefits, as well as the advantage of tapping into fundamental needs appropriate to the target audience: in this case the need for 'closeness' expressed through nurturing.

Relevance

What does 'relevance' mean? It may mean one of two things:

- it can meet my rational or emotional needs and is an acceptable price;
- practically, I have the opportunity to consider buying it.

It is more about the type of product or service that is offered than about how well that promise is delivered. It might be, for example, a question of:

Am I interested in . . .
a spreadable butter?
a toothpaste that protects gums?
a fixed rate mortgage?

This may sound like a fixed concept, but the relevance of a brand ebbs and flows for each of us, particularly in a category where we buy a repertoire of brands to meet different needs on different occasions.

The judgement of relevance is becoming increasingly flexible. Most markets are losing their neat structure, as new products or services come in which combine the benefits of previously incompatible sectors. The butter and margarine category used to be neatly structured, with clear groups such as dairy spreads, sunflower margarine, cooking margarine and so on. There used to be the belief that you could have good taste or good health, but not both in the same product. That perspective is now shifting, as brands such as 'I Can't Believe It's Not Butter' deliberately attack old assumptions.

It means that it is becoming less appropriate to see categories in terms of clear choice hierarchies that are consistent between consumers. The same applies to the concept of relevance, which is becoming less a question of a formula according to a combination of features, and more an holistic assessment of a brand.

Lack of relevance can mean being eliminated from consideration because of a knock-out factor, such as 'it is outside my price range' or 'it is not low in fat'. But more generally it is helpful to see it in a positive light, particularly for more emotional judgements, such as 'it suits me because it is fashionable/reliable/down to earth . . .'.

In some cases this does include a quality judgement: certain brands may not be considered relevant because they fail to meet the person's quality requirements. However, it seems to be more generally an issue of brand positioning rather than performance, even if this positioning is very loosely defined.

At first hearing it may sound a rather fixed concept, difficult to shift. This may be true to some extent, especially if the reasons behind a lack of relevance appear to be very specific tangible features. As with differentiation, there is always the option to change the rules of the game, encouraging people to see certain characteristics of a brand in a different light. Indeed, one measure of a good advert is to what extent it drives improved perception of the brand for differentiation and relevance.

Relevance is the biggest driver of brand equity in most quantitative models, certainly in explaining the current strength of a brand. It sets a maximum potential for a brand, in terms of the number of people who would consider buying it. This is interesting, since the natural expectation would be that quality would be more important than relevance in determining a brand's success. But once we appreciate that in the modern world consumers consider that most brands are able to do the job sufficiently well, it is easy to see why this is not the case. Brand choice has become less about concerns over how well the brand performs physically, or even performs in terms of status in the eyes of the neighbours. It is now much more a question of choice about what you feel suits *you* personally.

The importance of relevance is very visible in brand tracking studies, where it is often seen to decline for a brand that is in trouble, concurrent with or soon after differentiation declines.

This shows how fluid the relevance concept is, and how swiftly people's tastes may change, either as fashions change or as a result of longer-term trends. It is also important to remember that the user base for any brand is never constant. There are always new people joining and others departing. This is true despite the fact that we live in a world where age is becoming a much more flexible issue, and the strict divisions between the tastes and lifestyles of each age group are eroding. We do still get older and find that our tastes change.

Obviously some categories are very fashion-based, such as alcopops, while others seem to be with us for life, such as tea. If you look at the tea market in the UK you find a few striking characteristics. If you haven't started drinking tea by the age of 18 you will probably never start, and the brands seem to be the same as ever – for example PG Tips, whose Mr Shifter advert (the one where the chimps shift the piano) is one of the adverts most aired on British television. By contrast the alcopops market, with brands such as Hooch, is a clear example of 'here today, gone tomorrow'. They rise quickly, catch a wave of fashion, and then decline. If you're lucky you might get a five-year span, but in general the cycles are becoming shorter.

So, relevance can shift faster than you might expect. This is good news if you're looking to move your brand forward in some way, but not so good if you think you have found a nice position and simply want to stick with it. Many big brands become successful and then become complacent or over-familiar, and so gradually lose consumer interest. Then they lose not just differentiation but also the wide relevance that they enjoyed at their peak.

Relevance acts as a counterbalance to differentiation. Brands with very high relevance often have low differentiation, since they are aimed very broadly with few distinguishing features to exclude them from consideration. Conversely, brands with high differentiation tend to be targeted at a niche, and so have lower relevance.

Not surprisingly, the most successful brands are those which manage both, communicating differentiation without reducing their relevance, and continually innovating to maintain that relevance and differentiation against competition.

Performance

This means 'how well does the brand do the job for which you buy it?' This is mainly functional, contrasting with the more emotional component we have called 'empathy', discussed in the next section.

It appears to be automatic that better performance is a desirable thing for a brand. This is largely true for manufacturers' brands, though it is less clear for shops' own labels, which seem to need to be 'good enough', but do not necessarily need to be better than this. In fact, expectations of performance have become much more flexible over the years. The world used to be simpler, with manufacturers' branded products considered good quality, and supermarket own-label products expected to be inferior imitations. Some manufacturers used to proudly advertise that they did not supply products to be used in supermarket own-labels.

Now any brand can be good quality. We are less seduced by status, and we consciously distinguish between quality as functional effectiveness and quality in terms of style. Ambi-Pur is recognised as a stylish, sophisticated brand of air purifier, but that does not automatically mean people think it performs better than other brands. This recognises a concept of quality asserted by Robert Pirsig in his book *Zen and the Art of Motorcycle Maintenance*, where he noted the split between classical quality (functional/ structure) and romantic quality (style/presentation) and argued for their unification.

Brand equity factors tend to move slowly, but there can be striking exceptions when performance problems become visible and are talked about. Many examples are familiar, such as production difficulties or contamination that have happened to vehicles or food products.

These incidents make headline television news, so they quickly become very high profile. The accepted wisdom is therefore that when such problems occur, the best route forward is to admit them publicly and address them very visibly and dynamically. This means a large-scale recall of the product from the market, the bulk of which is perfectly OK but has to be withdrawn in order to guarantee catching all the defective items.

Even without specific emergency incidents, quality problems that become known and talked about will swiftly damage a brand's reputation. The example of Schlitz shows the dramatic decline that can result from quality problems. The story is described in detail in *Managing Brand Equity* by David Aaker. In short, cost-reduction changes were made to the product formulation, which were visible and criticised by the general public. Unfortunately this was not accepted and rectified by the Schlitz management until a few years later, by which time public confidence in the brand was so dented that the sales decline could not be reversed, despite new quality improvements that could be clearly demonstrated.

It is interesting to note that the swift action of withdrawing product following an emergency incident seems, generally, to allow the brand to recover relatively quickly. In this case people have short memories, or perhaps they consider that the company has acted decisively on a problem that may have been only partly its fault. As individual customers we tend to react the same way if we have to make a complaint to a company about poor service or a defective product. Our dissatisfaction can actually be turned round into a higher level of satisfaction than before the incident happened, if the company impresses us with its reaction to our complaint.

The same does not seem to be true in situations like the Schlitz example. The company is visibly responsible, and if not seen to act then the negative feeling will escalate. In this case people have long memories, so much so that even doubly strong remedial action at the wrong time will be too late.

Empathy

Empathy represents the emotional side to quality, a complement to the 'performance' side. To some extent it goes with relationship building at the higher levels of the needs map, whereas performance tends to emphasise the lower levels of the map. It means an emotional connection with a customer, a feeling of closeness and liking the brand. Some commentators on brand health would use a word such as 'bonding' to describe it. However, this type of language risks implying that the consumer cannot escape from the brand. Given the proliferation of choice in almost every category, this idea of inescapability seems inappropriate today. Or at least, any bonding may be temporary.

An emotional bond, or trust from your customer, is easily broken if a brand fails to live up to your claims. If you are going to claim green or ethical credentials, for example, beware of being exposed for failing to match up to the standards people will expect. And remember that it is all a question of public perception, which may in many cases be highly subjective, emotional and possibly ill-informed. If a bank takes a strong stance about being fair to customers, it will be judged on its perceived fairness according to the rules of consumers. The bank may try to claim that the application of small charges for use of competitors' cashpoint machines is reasonable, and a tiny issue compared to all the other positives it provides, but this may not be the basis for the public's judgement.

There is a certainly a strong wave of opinion that building a relationship with your customers is one of the most important brand-building activities of the modern world. It comes partly from a reaction against the aspiration that characterised the second age of branding, and implied a distance between brand and customer, together with a style of communication that talked down. This could be described as an adult–child or master–pupil form of relationship.

The new era sees brands becoming much more accessible in all areas. In his book *The New Marketing Manifesto*, John Grant presents this as the most important rule of new marketing, exhorting brands to 'get up close and personal'. Alan Mitchell describes it as 'helping buyers buy instead of sellers sell' in his book *Right Side Up*. The new mode of communication aims at a relationship of equals and empathy between the brand and its customers. You can observe this in everyday life, as well as in the mechanisms of marketing. Take banks as an example. Not so long ago a customer might be summoned to see his bank manager. This usually meant something unpleasant. Even in a survey 15 years ago to identify drivers of satisfaction, we found that 'accessibility of the manager' had a negative influence – the more the manager was visible and available, the less satisfied would be the customer.

Now it is different. We mentioned earlier the Midland Bank advert (before HSBC), where a 'normal' 30-year-old man goes in to see the manager, and tells him what he wants from a bank account. The customer is shown to be the one in control, not the brand or its representative, the bank manager. For an even more extreme example, look at the changes in presentation style of the Royal family – once waving politely from a distant balcony or the interior of a vehicle, now meeting and chatting face-to-face with people. Everyone is trying to build relationships.

Popularity

You can explain a large part of desire for a brand (its equity) in terms of the components described above: differentiation, relevance, performance, empathy and familiarity. But something is still missing. One noticeable thing about the list is its emphasis on a personal assessment, e.g. 'I think it performs well', or 'It is relevant to me'.

In a sense, popularity is about your perception of other people's opinions, whereas performance and empathy are about your own rational and emotional opinion of a brand. Popularity is a force in brand building, since people often choose a brand because of the security of knowing that lots of other people buy it: 'All those other people can't be wrong'. Of course, this makes it practically a quick, easy choice, as well as carrying emotional security.

Care is required with manipulating this concept in marketing. Too much popularity is a negative thing, if not supported by good brand promise in terms of differentiation and relevance, and good quality delivery. Also, for exclusivity-based brands, popularity is something to benefit from very cautiously but avoid cultivating.

A variation used in some models is to talk about 'perceived to be growing in popularity' rather than simply 'popular', which may be a static state. The two are therefore likely to be different. Indeed, once you've become popular, you're unlikely to have room still to be growing in popularity.

Arguably, both concepts suffer from the difficulty that they appear hard to act on and use as marketing levers. You can, however, think of cases such as Coca-Cola, whose massive visibility will drive a perception of popularity – at one time Coca-Cola had miles and miles of billboards in the USA. Think also of easyJet's adverts pointing out that they are the most popular airline in Ulster, presumably aimed at overcoming the impression that they should be viewed as a niche player, only for low budget travellers. Then remember the British Airways slogan, 'The world's favourite airline', and you realise that lots of brands try to act on this popularity dimension. You can also see how some brands manage to cultivate an image of being sought after by those 'in the know', which might lead to a perception of growing in popularity.

Given the choice between the two concepts, the 'simple' popularity dimension seems more consistently and widely relevant than the growth in popularity alternative. If you want to explain the success of big brands, the 'growth in popularity' version will not help. For growing niche brands, you will probably find their growing success is better explained by combinations of the other factors, led by differentiation.

Combinations of the Main Building Blocks

Figure 3.2 draws attention to various combinations of the six building blocks.

One problem particularly encountered here is the use of language. We are dealing with what are often referred to as 'fat words' – words that are potentially rich in meaning since they synthesise many things, but run the risk of different interpretations by different people, according to which aspect they lean on. All of the equity components under discussion suffer from this problem, though arguably some more than others. They can be very difficult to translate reliably if you are working on international brands.

Potential (Differentiation and Relevance)

This is a particularly important combination. We can create a total score for a brand for its combination of relevance and differentiation, which

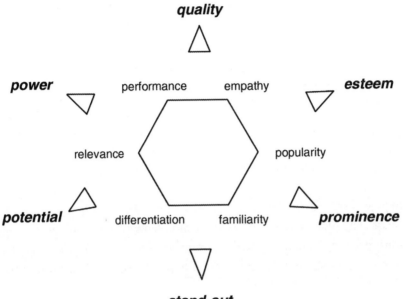

Figure 3.2 Combinations of equity building blocks

serves as a good indicator of the brand's potential. If it exhibits a positioning with a wide potential audience (relevance) and at the same time has something new to offer consumers (differentiation), then it has a great chance of future success. There is no barrier to attracting people to try it.

This is frequently a characteristic of brands that are on their way up: they manage to display high potential, but have not yet managed to establish a high position on the other equity components. They have not been around long enough to have become popular, to have established deep familiarity, for their performance qualities to have been discovered, or for a strong empathy to have been built with a large customer base.

Power (Relevance and Performance)

When you take strong performance delivery, linked to widely relevant consumer needs, you have the combination of 'power'. The brand is not simply good at what it does, it is also focused on the areas with the widest appeal. This combination therefore characterises a brand very focused on delivery in the right area.

When long-term market leaders begin to decline, it is often noticeable that their relevance has dropped. Their performance often remains high, but the problem is that they are no longer focused on the most important consumer needs for their category.

Quality (Performance and Empathy)

Quality is a dangerous word, along with words such as equity and loyalty. At least with equity, you know it's a jargon word and will need careful definition before you can make any sensible use of it. The word quality is more dangerous since it's in everyday use, so we all think we know what it means.

Here we avoid some of the pitfalls by defining it as a combination of performance and empathy. It therefore means, as a synthesis, that the brand is connecting well with the consumer on both an emotional and a functional level.

In practice, in research studies it can be hard to distinguish clearly between these two aspects of quality. That is to say, brands are generally perceived well on both aspects, or poorly on both aspects. This is more the case than for the combination of relevance and performance, where we often find niche brands that deliver high performance but operate in an area of their category which has low relevance; and it is even more extreme for the combination of differentiation and relevance, where the two are often in opposition.

Esteem (Empathy and Popularity)

This is the combination indicating brands that are much loved and held in high regard. It means that you personally feel close to the brand (empathy) and you also think that other people do so as well (popularity). It distinguishes those brands with a strong public reputation from brands that display high popularity but lower empathy, which are mass-market brands meeting a wide audience but not delivering particularly high quality.

Esteem contrasts with its opposite in Figure 3.2, namely potential. On the one hand we have brands that are potentially on the way up, that are new discoveries and stars of the future. On the other hand, we have today's big success stories.

Prominence (Popularity and Familiarity)

Here we find the combination that describes how well known the brand is, or the ubiquity of the brand. It highlights brands that seem to be everywhere and to have been around for a long time. It sits opposite the combination of power, which in contrast is all about content. Prominence tells you nothing about the brand's effectiveness or usefulness for your purpose. Prominent brands can easily be living on past glories. Conversely, a brand with lots of 'power' will under-achieve if people do not know enough about it, if it is not sufficiently visible and prominent.

Stand-out (Familiarity and Differentiation)

High familiarity tells us that the brand is known for something, and differentiation tells us that this something is distinct from other brands. This therefore synthesises into a concept of 'stand-out'. Brands with high stand-out will be ones that people feel able to describe or put a label on: 'I know that brand, it's the one that does X'.

The stand-out combination contrasts with its opposite, the combination of performance and empathy that creates quality. Stand-out is all about saying something, regardless of whether it is good or bad. Quality is all about delivering that something.

Other Combinations

As well as the six combinations just discussed, we can look at bigger groupings. The most important of these are those on the left of Figure 3.2

(differentiation, relevance and performance) versus the ones on the right (empathy, popularity and familiarity). Terms such as 'brand strength' are often used for the left, and 'brand stature' for the right. The precise findings from different equity models vary, but one of their general themes is that the balance between strength and stature is a good indicator of future success for a brand. The clearest finding is that brands on the way down, or at risk of going down, tend to be higher on stature than on strength.

Another triplet of interest is the grouping of differentiation, familiarity and popularity. For this you might apply a label of 'salience', as it clearly relates to getting your brand talked about. The opposite set of three is about doing the job required, covering relevance, performance and empathy. It is about quality in the right area for you. And the final pairing would be something like 'opinion' (combining performance, empathy and popularity) versus 'clarity' (meaning relevance, differentiation and familiarity).

One of the reasons for contrasting all these opposites is to highlight that successful brands need to do well on all these components. The opposites are not choices; they are balanced necessities. If your brand falls down on one or more of them, then either it will limit your future growth, or it will indicate a problem area to address.

4

Touchpoints and Brand Physique

A Framework for Physique, Perceptions, Needs and Touchpoints

A problem familiar to any experienced market researcher is the abundance of different terms for describing aspects of brands. I've already used quite a few in this book, such as associations, perceptions and equity, and there are more to come in the rest of the book.

The terminology can be very confusing. Dealing with many companies, we find different words used for more or less the same thing, and the same words used to mean different things. This seems particularly noticeable when attempting to describe some of the properties of a brand, when phrases such as brand essence, brand identity or brand physique are used.

Part of the issue is that particular words imply not just a definition of something, but also a mental model or way of viewing the subject. A phrase such as 'brand essence' tends to come from a brand manager's perspective, with an underlying implication of properties of a brand that exist independently of any consumer perspective. As a researcher, I find I use language that draws on the consumer perspective, promoting a point of view that the brand only really exists in the mind of consumers. Recognising this, in this chapter we will talk about two concepts, the brand's physique and touchpoints with the consumer, both of which emphasise the consumer's side of the story.

There are many complex models for describing our relationship with brands, but Figure 4.1 presents a simple framework for illustrating the role of touchpoints and brand physique in how we experience and perceive brands, taking a brand of whisky as an example.

The Brand's Physique

On the left of the figure are listed some elements of the brand's physique, such as its Scottish origin and the number of years the product is matured.

In Chapter 1 we talked about the 'associations' that an individual has with a brand, and illustrated how these covered a spectrum: at one end very personal, unique associations such as an event in your life that connects with the brand; at the other end associations held by many people, such as a specific colour that is consistently visible in the product, the service or its marketing. These more common associations can be called the 'brand physique'.

The physique therefore includes colours, shapes, logos, slogans, characters, product features, images and so on. These can be factual information, such as the alcohol content of the product, or they can be much less tangible, such as an image or impression of sunshine. Some marketing people would call it the 'reasons to believe' in the brand, meaning the substance that underpins perceptions of the brand.

If the same association is held by the majority of people, such as the duck shape for the brand Toilet Duck, then it is indisputably part of the physique. These sorts of associations are powerful hooks for brand recognition and familiarity. Other associations are less clearly consistent between people, such as the concept of 'waiting' for the Guinness brand, and they may be present in the minds of fewer people, so there is more debate about whether they are part of the physique. Although less clearly part of the physique, these sorts of elements can be more powerful for marketing purposes since they are more evocative and flexible. They serve less to trigger recognition and more to create a platform for conveying the meaning of the brand.

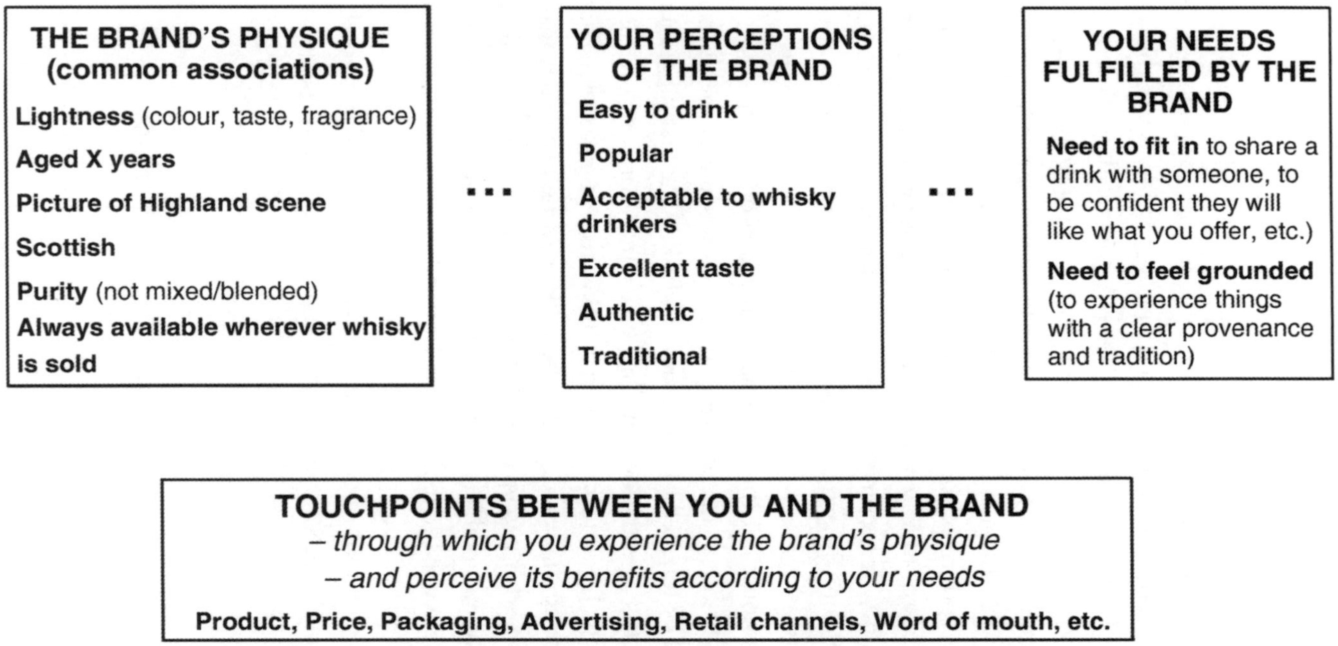

THE BRAND'S PHYSIQUE (common associations)

Lightness (colour, taste, fragrance)

Aged X years

Picture of Highland scene

Scottish

Purity (not mixed/blended)

Always available wherever whisky is sold

■ ■ ■

YOUR PERCEPTIONS OF THE BRAND

Easy to drink

Popular

Acceptable to whisky drinkers

Excellent taste

Authentic

Traditional

■ ■ ■

YOUR NEEDS FULFILLED BY THE BRAND

Need to fit in to share a drink with someone, to be confident they will like what you offer, etc.)

Need to feel grounded (to experience things with a clear provenance and tradition)

TOUCHPOINTS BETWEEN YOU AND THE BRAND
– *through which you experience the brand's physique*
– *and perceive its benefits according to your needs*

Product, Price, Packaging, Advertising, Retail channels, Word of mouth, etc.

Figure 4.1 Whisky brand profile for physique, perceptions, needs and touchpoints

The physique is relatively objective, in the sense that it contains no judgement about whether something is good or bad. For example, the Scottish origin for the whisky brand might be very positive for some people and very negative for others. Also, many of the subtle elements of the physique will be interpreted in varying ways. Some people may gain an impression of lightness for our example brand of whisky, since they compare it with other heavier whiskies they have experienced, while other people feel it is heavy, since they compare it with other sorts of products.

So, each brand has a physique that represents the overlap of everyone's associations with the brand, and this provides the basis or the substance for common perceptions of the brand. We might judge it to be an acceptable brand to serve to other whisky drinkers, on the basis of its lightness and wide availability. It becomes apparent here that it can be hard to separate the physique from the perceptions. It is clear enough if the item is factual such as 'Scottish' (physique), or if it is a definite benefit such as 'excellent taste' (perception), but there is a large grey area of overlap.

On the right-hand side of Figure 4.1 we show some of the deeper needs which would be touched by this brand of whisky. The first suggestion is the need to fit in, a variation on the 'love' and 'harmony' needs in the universal map. In connection with whisky, this might mean choosing a brand you are confident someone else will like when you offer it to them. This connects with perceptions of the brand being easy to drink, popular and generally acceptable to whisky drinkers. Similarly, there may be a connection to a need to feel grounded, articulated as a desire to experience things which have a clear provenance and tradition. This is picked up by the brand perceptions of authenticity and tradition, and is traceable back to the physique components of purity (not blended) and specific place of origin.

Touchpoints Between You and the Brand

The term 'touchpoints' means all the contexts in which we come into contact with the brand. It covers the vehicles or circumstances through which we experience the brand physique. It ranges over many aspects, including the product or service, the price, packaging, advertising, word of mouth, and so on.

Touchpoints fall into two broad groupings: first-hand experience through using the brand, and communications about the brand. This split is emphasised through the structure of most companies, where 'first-hand experience' is the responsibility of the product management or service delivery departments, while communication is the responsibility of the marketing department.

Tangible elements of the brand's physique are often present in the same way across as many of the touchpoints as possible. A services brand will show its logo in its high street branches, in its advertising and in all its written communications with customers. Less tangible parts of the physique may be evoked across the touchpoints in more complementary ways. For example, the purity of the whisky can be emphasised by the clarity of the liquid, the packaging, the advertising and even the types of retail channel where it can be found. Indeed, this reinforcement may be necessary to establish in people's minds some of the less tangible parts of the physique.

Putting it all together, the task of the brand manager is to use all the touchpoints to create a physique for the brand in people's minds. This sounds manageable, but the combination of experience of touchpoints is specific to each person. The brand manager has only limited control over each touchpoint, and in some cases no control at all. The way people use any brand will vary, as will their exposure and reaction to any communication about the brand.

The Influence of each Touchpoint

The Relative Importance of each Touchpoint

A frequent issue is the importance of each touchpoint in influencing the success of the brand. How much influence is exerted by the communications, how much through using the brand, and how much by indirect channels such as word-of-mouth and general media coverage?

Obviously, direct experience of the product or service only plays a part for existing buyers or customers of the brand. Here the indications are that this experience has the majority influence, as would be expected. But communications also account for part of it, as does word-of-mouth and media coverage.

A few years ago a study for a major UK bank revealed that around 80 per cent of future willingness to deal with the bank was explained by the experience of using the products and the service. The rest was driven equally by managed communications (mainly TV advertising) and by unmanaged communications (word-of-mouth and media reports about the company). Unfortunately the media coverage at the time was largely negative, so this effect virtually cancelled out the positive effect of the advertising.

It is equally of interest to know which equity building blocks are driven by each marketing lever. Here the indications are that relevance and quality judgements are particularly driven by direct product or service experience, while for differentiation the influence of advertising increases and usage diminishes.

This latter point is perhaps the most interesting. It highlights that competing brands tend to appear similar when we use them, but that their advertising has the scope to be very distinctive. Case histories show that advertising is able to make a clear difference to the total appeal of a brand, even when the direct experience is almost identical. This does not seem surprising for extreme cases, such as the impact a few years ago of the famous advertising for Tango, at that time a poorly differentiated product in the UK soft drinks category. More interesting is the fact that we see good, mainstream advertising able to make a brand distinctive.

How People's Needs Connect with each Touchpoint

In the same way that one element of the brand physique may be carried across many different touchpoints, we also often find that one consumer need is met through a combination of touchpoints. Figure 4.2 illustrates this interaction.

COMPANY PERSPECTIVE

Touchpoints with the customer or potential customer

CUSTOMER PERSPECTIVE: NEEDS	Product	Staff	Environment (store/branch)	Communication (adverts, PR)
Innovation	New/interesting products			
Excitement	Fun/exciting products			Adverts suggest excitement
Individuality		Staff treat me as an individual		
Status		Staff make me feel important		
Care			Nice décor/ambience	Adverts suggest caring company
Security	Trust the products	Staff are reassuring		
Ease		Helpful staff		
Information	Good instructions		Good signage	
Speed		Fast staff	Short queues	
Effectiveness		Knowledgeable staff		
Reliability	Products don't break	Staff don't make mistakes		
Accessibility	Products in stock	Availability of staff		

Relationship ←——————→ Functional

Customer service is delivered through specific details, such as 'queue length'. These are a combination of the touchpoint and the customer need(s) it aims to fulfil.

Figure 4.2 Needs and touchpoints

On the left-hand side of the chart is the customer, with his needs. Taking a retail brand as an example, these needs range from functional (e.g. speed and not making mistakes), through to emotional (e.g. excitement). At the top of the chart are shown the touchpoints, such as the products, the staff, the store design and the advertising.

At the intersection of the two we find perception attributes. These may mostly be viewed as a combination of the need and the touchpoint. The attribute 'short queues' combines the need for speed and the touchpoint of the checkouts.

This chart shows how consumers derive their fulfilment of each of their needs from across all the touchpoints, although each touchpoint varies in importance. The need for speed will be fulfilled through the combined effect of good store layout, signposting, efficient staff, number of checkouts open, and so on. As well as these in-store experiences, advertising may help with advance information.

One of the common weaknesses encountered in market research studies is that they emphasise vertical analysis in this figure. For example, well trained staff tend to do most things well, while badly trained staff will do the reverse. This causes the mathematical patterns in the data to tend to show the vertical connections, and this happens regardless of which sophisticated mathematical technique is used. This is fine on one hand, since it tells the company what the customer thinks of each touchpoint, which is helpful for managing each internal system, but the drawback is that it loses sight of the fulfilment of consumers' underlying needs as a whole – which is the real determinant of the brand's success.

This highlights another common problem. There is often a marked separation between different departments in a company. For example, marketing people show no interest in what happens with service delivery, while service people take no part in discussions about marketing. It is important that different touchpoints work together to define and communicate a consistent identity for the brand. It is well known that advertising and sponsorship work best when they are used in tandem, one supporting the other. Equally, it is important that marketing communicates ideas about the brand that will fit with direct experience of the product or service. Problems arise when advertising sets up expectations about the brand that are actually contradicted by the customer experience.

This does not mean that every marketing channel should shout the same message. Each has specific characteristics that point to them being used to best effect in different ways and for different purposes.

The figure also reveals another reason why there is often a separation in the mind of the company between product/service and brand. All the boxes in the chart are likely to contain something, but generally functional needs will be connected to first-hand experience, while emotional or relationship needs will be more connected to communications vehicles. This can lead to the impression that 'the brand' means the higher emotional stuff, conveyed by the advertising, separate from the functional needs fulfilled by product and service delivery. This false split is compounded by the ways many research programmes are organised, divided between a 'customer satisfaction study' and a 'brand and advertising study'. The truth is that advertising *can* change people's reactions to the functional experience, and that product and service experiences *do* contribute to the fulfilment of emotional as well as functional needs.

Customer Satisfaction

Customer satisfaction plays a very big part in brand success. You would thus expect the subject to be well understood, but its usefulness is frequently challenged and there are many misconceptions about how it works. The following sections discuss this issue.

Description, Opinion or Satisfaction

First let's draw attention to some important distinctions between the three concepts of description, opinion and satisfaction. Consider the example in Figure 4.3.

Imagine a customer uses a five-star hotel and a one-star hotel. Suppose she experiences a waiting time of three minutes to pay her bill in the

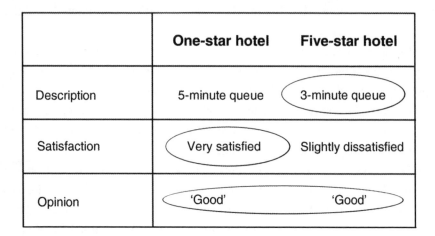

Figure 4.3 Description, opinion and satisfaction

upmarket hotel and five minutes in the basic hotel. This is an objective description of the service, and on this measure the five-star hotel performs slightly better.

Now ask the customer about her satisfaction level in each case. Here we might find that she is slightly dissatisfied with the five-star hotel, since she feels she should get a better service when she is paying such a high price. Conversely, she may be completely satisfied with the one-star hotel, since she has lower expectations of it. So now we have the reverse situation. The basic establishment generates higher satisfaction, despite delivering objectively the poorer service.

Finally, imagine we had asked the customer her 'opinion' of the speed of paying the bill. In answer to this question she might have responded that it was 'good' in both cases. Opinion ratings are one of the most common questions in the whole of quantitative market research, yet among the hardest to pin down in their meaning. They appear in one sense to be asking for an objective report, and therefore should be close to a factual description of the service delivery. However, at the same time they are undoubtedly subjective (they are asking *me* what *I* think of it), and so in this respect they are close to the satisfaction question.

The net result is that each of the three types of measurement potentially leads to different conclusions. According to one approach, the basic hotel seemed better, by another method the expensive hotel seemed better, and by a third approach they were both judged to be equal.

The three approaches differ in their degree of subjectivity and the frame of reference in each case. To some degree, of course, the answer to every type of question risks being subjective. Even on something tangible like waiting time, people will report it slightly inaccurately, according to how they felt about it. Their reports are still valuable information, but not perfect. If they feel happy they may tend to underestimate the time slightly, whereas if they were unhappy they may overestimate it a little.

The point of all these distinctions is that these different forms of measurement highlight quite different things, with different implications for brand success and the management of product and service delivery. Of the three, we find that customer retention, and hence brand success, is most strongly a function of satisfaction. This is understandable, since it is closest to the customer and his own needs, but it is not easily linked back to the actual service delivered. This is one reason why companies find it hard to adopt a genuinely customer-centric point of view, and tend to slide back to a company-centric point of view when setting standards for service implementation.

A striking example of one company that managed to change its focus is British Airways. At one time its service was focused on very manageable, definable practicalities, such as the speed of providing meals to passengers after take-off. But this was not a high priority need for customers, and satisfaction improved when attention was focused more on friendly service – which is harder to define and to set standards, but more important.

Our Frame of Reference

While the time spent waiting to pay a bill can be measured reasonably objectively, many experiences are undoubtedly in the eye, ear, nose or mouth of the beholder. This is very visible in the results we obtain in blind versus branded tests of food products. A strong brand such as Kellogg's Cornflakes will achieve much higher ratings when tested in the branded packaging than in the blind packaging, where all indications of the branding have been removed. This is one illustration of how branding is considered to change the experience, or changes people's perception or judgement of their experience.

Another important consideration is the truth that one man's drink is another man's poison. There is no such thing as objective judgement. *You* may think a queue of 10 minutes in a post office is fine, while *I* may think it is scandalous. We all bring our own frame of reference to each judgement we make.

This seems obvious when presented like this, but it is often forgotten when companies judge their service delivery standards. Staff may consider that an interval of three days between placement and delivery of an order is a great achievement, for which the customer should feel grateful. But the customer is unaware of the processes involved, and it's not his problem. He judges it against his own personal frame of reference, which might include totally different industries and situations. Or he might simply need the item delivered in under three days, and this will affect his opinions about the service.

Brand communications may set up expectations which will affect how the product or service is judged. A few years ago, the supermarket Tesco began to emphasise customer service and promised a 'one-in-front' policy: if there was more than one person in front of you at the checkout, it would endeavour to open more checkouts. This sort of statement sets up expectations, and your brand will be judged accordingly. Falling short of that benchmark will create greater dissatisfaction for your brand than it would for competitors, if they have not made such claims. In the case of Tesco, they did succeed in delivering that service, and reaped the reward.

The key, obvious, principle is that it is our own personal reaction, our satisfaction, which is most likely to drive our future use of the brand. People may argue about how we should measure satisfaction, but it seems clear that this concept is closer to influencing your overall attitude and behaviour than any more objective measure, such as factual observations of queue length. Certainly, other factors also come into play, such as your views of other brands and your natural mobility or inertia – whether you can be bothered to move, regardless of whether you are satisfied – but satisfaction is a key driver of future behaviour and brand success.

Revising our Expectations

Objectively, standards of product quality and many aspects of service delivery have improved immeasurably over the years, but everyone reports that levels of satisfaction have remained constant, despite these improvements.

We simply redefine our expectations. We move the goalposts. This may well happen with all types of question asking people to judge things, but it is most often reported as a problem with satisfaction studies. It is as if we expect people to judge service delivery against some notional, objective, reasonable benchmark, just because it seems functional, whereas we accept readily that emotional or intangible things will be judged more vaguely or personally. Companies are forever setting target improvements on customer satisfaction in ways they would never dream of doing for other measures of how well their brand is performing.

Customer Acquisition and Retention

All this discussion of the importance of customer satisfaction might be taken to imply that it is the only factor in a customer's judgement of a brand they use. But remember the bank example, which suggested in that instance that 80 per cent of the action was attributable to customer satisfaction and the remaining 20 per cent to communications, ignoring any cross-over influence between the two.

It is false dichotomous thinking that leads to statements such as, 'It is the brand that is responsible for customer acquisition, and satisfaction that is responsible for customer retention'. No it isn't. Existing customers tell other people about their experiences, good and bad, so satisfaction affects acquisition, and existing customers absorb the brand values in ways that non-customers don't even come close to. In fact, they sometimes go far beyond the values that the brand manager tries to promote.

Beauty is in the eye of the beholder. An owner of a Volvo 330 once said to me: 'You know, the Volvo 330 is a very stylish car'. Now, the 330 may have had many virtues, but it would be a surprise if style was high on the list in most people's judgement. This guy wasn't just a satisfied customer, he really believed in the whole brand.

Identifying Improvements

If you can improve customer satisfaction relative to your competitors, then you will improve your brand equity and your brand's success. This line of thinking naturally leads to an analysis of the drivers of satisfaction, and plans for how performance on these may be improved. This is great if you achieve it, but it can have limitations. It is like being in a bicycle race, and trying to find ways of making your bike go faster. You might manage this, perhaps by pedalling faster or streamlining the design. This is the equivalent of improvements you might identify and act on through conventional customer satisfaction research.

However, there may come a point where you cannot pedal any faster, or you cannot overtake the competition in this way. In this sort of situation you need to think 'out of the box'. You need a motorbike instead of a bicycle. Use the diagram of needs versus touchpoints to see what fundamental needs are held by your customers, and how these are being fulfilled by the combination of different touchpoints. This may lead to new ideas about how to improve service, since it can lift you out of the current internal mechanisms, allowing you to see them from a new angle.

Supermarkets now have home delivery services and self-scanning, which tackle the customer's need for speed in different ways. Imagine a different service for people *really* in a hurry, where they could telephone the shop with a take-away order for up to 10 items, and then collect it a few minutes later on their way home, without any waiting at all.

Key Events, Delight and Disaster

The words 'satisfaction' and 'dissatisfaction' carry a relatively low amount of emotion. Neither of them sound strong enough to indicate a call to action;

so they only tell part of the story in understanding customers' reaction to their experiences.

The strongest triggers to action happen when the emotions are engaged more strongly, when we are delighted or angry. Delight causes the positive action of telling the good news to other people and being open to using the brand more often or more widely. Anger causes the negative action of telling the bad news to other people and defecting from the brand or company.

Delight and anger are likely to come from occasional, significant events. Most customer experience falls within safe, familiar boundaries, which causes us to be, on balance, relatively satisfied or dissatisfied. But the big reactions tend to come from the unexpected.

Communications

A great deal has been written and spoken about the way advertising works, but rarely is it contrasted with the effects of the brand usage experience. Given everything said so far about the importance of the combined effects on the consumer of all the touchpoints with a brand, let's examine the nature of advertising and other communications from this point of view.

Freedom vs Constraint

Overall, there is often a marked gulf, even a sense of hostility and mutual incomprehension, between the marketing department and the product or customer service department. This seems particularly true in service companies, although you can also find it in manufacturers of packaged goods.

Customer service people may believe that they are the ones doing the real job of delivering the product, providing the service and dealing with real customers. They see advertising as a sort of glossy add-on, potentially irresponsible and unaccountable, and dealing with intangibles. Meanwhile, the marketing and advertising people often believe themselves to be the ones responsible for creating the brand, and sometimes seem to consider customer service as an irritating constraint.

This is an unfortunate point of view, but it does highlight one of the genuine differences between the two. Advertising enjoys a freedom in what it says and how it says it, whereas customer service is constrained by the tough practical challenge of delivering the product or service. Advertising is very manoeuvrable – there is often little connection between the style or content of successive advertising campaigns, whereas it is extremely difficult to make major changes to the internal structures responsible for service delivery.

These freedoms allow advertising potentially to convey any association or impression desired by the company. Furthermore, it appears to be a fairly manageable freedom. People will have different reactions to an advert, and take away varying impressions of the brand, but you can largely anticipate these by research before airing the advert. Advertising rarely suffers from the unfortunate mistakes and bad experiences that customer service has to cope with.

Creativity vs Safety

The freedom of advertising extends to a wide variety of creative approaches. Advertising can teach, tell stories, seduce, entertain, tempt, tease, challenge, shock and make you laugh. Customer service might also make you laugh, but mainly in situations when you feel like crying.

True, we talk about the goal of *delighting* customers, but the first objective is more likely to be avoidance of the jarring experience. Delivery of the product/service aims mainly to fit within safe boundaries, meeting or perhaps slightly exceeding expectations, but not trying to stand out. Meanwhile, advertising is in the business of creating those expectations and definitely standing out.

As brands become closer in terms of what they deliver, it seems that it is increasingly difficult for customer service to do anything very dramatic, except when it delivers a bad experience. The trend is towards similarity between brands. Conversely, advertising is perpetually looking for ways to stand out and be different. It does this for two reasons: to gain attention in the face of competition, and to communicate a reason to consider one brand rather than another. Those may sound like active, rational processes by the consumer, but they are more than this. The attention may be subliminal instead of highly conscious, and the advert content may not be of the type that is easy for people to recall. The reason to consider the brand may be nothing more than a vague connection to a feeling, a 'soft' notion that you have some sense of what this brand is about, simply because it has some associations in your mind.

Disruption vs Status Quo

In the brand usage experience, people judge the 'performance' of the brand according to the accepted rules of the game. Advertising has the opportunity to overturn those rules before you get to that stage. It can encourage people to think differently, to see something in a different light, not just a better light, and to turn a potential drawback into a positive. We gave examples of this earlier, with the Guinness and Smash adverts.

This contrasts with brand usage and customer satisfaction. Here, unexpected surprises tend to be avoided. When they do happen they are likely to be an extension of good service, not a completely different way of doing things.

Low vs High Involvement

Having said that the experience of using the product or service typically sits within safe boundaries, the big triggers happen at the extremes. You are very conscious and highly involved when the product or service falls short of your requirements. Far more people get worked up enough to complain about a service experience than to complain about an advert, whether to a friend, a company or an official body. Equally, one of the best single indicators of the health of a brand is the extent to which existing customers are delighted enough to recommend it to other people.

You have a real, active interest in the brand usage experience. You've either chosen the brand yourself or, worse, you've had the brand forced upon you by circumstance. Either way, you've doubtless paid some money and the outcome matters to you.

Advertising is different. It is likely to be lower involvement, particularly television advertising. In most cases people don't watch TV adverts consciously looking for information about the brand. Advert watching is a passive, low involvement activity, where the advert largely washes over you. You may pay conscious attention to some elements, but a lot of very good adverts convey their impressions far more subtly.

This all means that advertising, particularly TV advertising, works in mysterious ways, while customer service works in a pretty overt way. As a customer, you tend to know good service when you see it, but the same is not true for advertising.

Demonstration of Benefit

In some situations there are differences between brands which are effortlessly visible to the consumer. You really can see for yourself that American Airlines provide more legroom. In such a case, when the company is confident the feature will not be copied tomorrow by a competitor, it is good to tell the world and reinforce the message by advertising it; American Airlines put this message into their logo.

More often, though, the differences between brands are more subtle, either invisible or where judgement is heavily influenced by other factors. You may think a particular stomach pain remedy to be faster acting than another one, but you can't really test it yourself. You may think you can, but it is unlikely that you will take the necessary steps to conduct a scientific test, with the effects of the brand communication removed.

Processes to do with the human body are well known to respond to the power of communication. To give you another example, we once tested two versions of a well-known, high fibre breakfast cereal. One of them was higher in fibre, but a lighter colour. The fibre content was concealed from the testers. A few weeks later at the end of the test, they claimed the darker one had had the stronger laxative effect.

So the irony is that advertising is often better placed than brand usage to convey a point of difference. In some cases it might do this directly through endorsement by an authority, such as pet foods (top breeders), toothpaste (dentists) and cars (car magazines). This is becoming a less popular strategy, now that we prefer our brands to be more accessible rather than talking down to us. More common is the subtler version of using a celebrity whom we like, who may make direct comments about the product or simply associate himself with it.

Deeper Needs

Brand usage contributes to your judgement of whether the brand does the job you want. It may take a major role in this regarding functional delivery, but it becomes a supporter to advertising where the aim is to create strong and deep emotional associations. The famous 'orange hit' Tango adverts convey laddish fun. These fit well enough with the product characteristics – bright orange and fizzy – but you would be hard pushed to extract those connections without the advertising.

Generally, it seems that one of the strongest combinations is advertising connecting with a big, fundamental need, combined with a usage experience which has a few physical hooks to help convince us that the benefit is delivered.

Brand Linkage

One of the biggest challenges for advertising is brand linkage. Many adverts work hard and successfully to attract attention, communicate a specific message, encourage familiarity with an idea, an image or a branding device, but fail to establish a connection with the brand.

This is rarely an issue with direct experience of a product or service. You know who you are dealing with as a customer; you don't need to be reminded.

Sponsorship

Gone are the days when arts, sporting events and television programmes were chosen on a whim for sponsorship. Now it is recognised that these carry many powerful connections, which can help a brand strengthen or move its image. It overlaps with advertising, but has a few important distinctions. Many sponsorships are seen by the public as 'good' advertising, where the company is spending money in a way that is benefiting the public, in return for having its name aired. In this way it opens up some associations that advertising will struggle to deliver.

More important than the brand awareness it generates is likely to be the connection with the image of the activity or programme that is sponsored. If there is a natural fit, e.g. Mars with the London Marathon or Cadbury's with Coronation Street, then the association can be strong and long-lasting in consumers' minds. One potential drawback is that it creates a channel for transfer of *all* the image characteristics of the programme or event, so it may do many things you want, but also some others you don't want.

The history of previous sponsors creates a context which has to be broken for the new sponsor to register. If this is very strong, it could be almost like a new brand of toilet paper adopting a puppy in its adverts. It would only work if the connection to Andrex is successfully broken.

Most important of all, though, sponsorship will be most effective when it works in harmony with other touchpoints to tell a complete story about the brand.

Being Talked About

Advertising and sponsorship are sometimes referred to as 'managed communication'. This of course implies that they are under control of the company, which is true in the fact of their creation, but not so true in what consumers take out of them. Less controllable are 'unmanaged communications', by which we mean word-of-mouth and media coverage.

These are undeniably powerful, for good or ill. In one test case, the bad publicity concerning a major bank outweighed the good, heavy advertising expenditure. This was compounded because the company was being perceived to be unfair, thus contradicting the advertising, which suggested fairness and honesty.

In other more positive examples, the effect of positive content of an advert will be multiplied if the general public adopt it and talk about it. One of the notable successes of the Tango advert was the way it entered the culture of playgrounds, with children acting out the face-slapping. This is free publicity, and has a momentum all of its own, although what it says about the brand cannot be predicted.

Branding Devices

The expression 'branding devices' covers slogans, logos, pictures, colours, shapes, sounds, music, characters and people that are associated with a brand. They are key elements of the physique that act as a hook for brand recognition and identification, and therefore assist the impact of all forms of communication. Some brands seem almost completely defined by them, the advertising being mainly a vehicle for showing the branding device and the packaging showing the device very prominently. An example of this is the Toilet Duck.

Branding devices also contribute to the impressions people have of the brand. Colours and shapes carry implications of levels of style, energy, sophistication and so on. These are often very subtle or subconscious associations, and whole branches of research are devoted to them, such as semiotics.

To give the general flavour, but to avoid suggesting that there are fixed rules about these things, here are some suggestions about the types of image that might connect with each of the big needs in the universal map covered earlier.

- *Liberty*: light, airy images, such as clouds, kites, irregular shapes, whites, yellows;
- *Harmony*: soft, flowing shapes, such as gentle waves, soft blues, dreamy imagery;

- *Closeness*: folding in, enclosing, depth, deep blue, protective gestures, stillness, quiet;
- *Structure*: upright, straight lines, geometric, dark colours, square;
- *Challenge*: forceful shapes, red, strong colours, acute angles;
- *Excitement*: lightning forks, zigzag movements, scenes chopping and changing (like a pop video), loud, fast.

The devices work best when the brand values accord with them, e.g. 'The future's bright, the future's Orange'. More volatile is the use of well-known personalities as vehicles for association with the brand. These can be fantastic when the connection is a positive one, but may easily change if the person does something that sours their image with the public. To illustrate these various points, Figure 4.4 shows a list of well-known advertising slogans.

Where do you want to go to today?	**MICROSOFT**
Connecting people	**NOKIA**
The car in front is a . . .	**TOYOTA**
Don't leave home without it.	**AMEX**
The best a man can get.	**GILLETTE**
The ultimate driving machine.	**BMW**
Just do it!	**NIKE**
No-one does chicken like . . .	**KFC (Kentucky Fried Chicken)**
Latin spirit in every one.	**BACARDI**
Good things come to those who wait.	**GUINNESS**
No . . ., no comment	**FT (Financial Times)**
United Colours of	**BENETTON**
It's good to talk.	**BT (British Telecom)**

Figure 4.4 Current well-known advertising slogans

Examining the list, we can draw the following observations about characteristics that make a good slogan:

- long and consistent use, e.g. 'No FT, no comment'
- integrated with advert message, e.g. 'It's good to talk'
- brand connection in meaning, e.g. 'Latin spirit in every one'
- brand connection in rhyme, e.g. 'The best a man can get'
- tapping a fundamental need, e.g. 'Just do it' tapping into the need for Challenge.

We may apply the same analysis to logos, drawing very similar conclusions. Two main themes emerge: integration with other elements, and consistent use. In the latter, there is clearly a danger in switching branding devices too frequently or carrying too many at once. You risk losing the simple hook for brand recognition and lowering consumer identification with the brand because it becomes less clear what the brand stands for.

5

Segmentation and Targeting: Where should you Aim?

Why Aim for Target Segments?

Ten to twenty years ago, lots of 'segmentation studies' in market research were carried out. These asked how to find a way of classifying buyers of a category into different types (segments). This could be based on a number of aspects, such as their attitudes to the category, their usage behaviour, the way they choose between brands, and their broader lifestyle or attitudes to life.

These studies are less common now, or at least they are taking on a somewhat different form, so in this chapter we look at the role of segmentation and the most useful ways of doing it.

A lot of time is still spent by marketers and market researchers on analysing the structure of markets, defining segments and developing strategies for targeting each segment. Why is this done? Why not design a universal product and market it to everyone?

One immediate answer is portfolio management. A company with multiple brands or products in a market usually prefers not to have them competing against each other (although there are exceptions). They achieve the best success through aiming the brands at different market segments.

A broader reason, applicable to brands in general, is the decline of ubiquity. The proliferation of products has encouraged greater choice and discrimination. Consumers expect to find products and services designed to be appropriate for specific situations, needs and people, and indeed they find them. It is a sweeping statement, but generally a product designed for a narrower set of needs or situations will perform better, when judged in the appropriate context, than a product that is designed to be more multi-purpose. The multi-purpose product therefore risks coming a poor second across many market segments, whereas the specialist product can come first in one segment and not worry about the others. The targeted strategy therefore typically stands a greater chance of success, albeit within a specific segment which may limit its total potential.

This all implies a brand positioning based on meeting a small number of needs exceptionally well, at the expense of meeting other needs. However, this must be balanced against the fact that really successful brands make an art of reconciling *apparent* opposites. Witness the example of Coca-Cola and Guinness, which seem to maintain an up-to-date image in conjunction with a strong heritage – a merging of modernity and tradition in the concept of timelessness.

Another argument against specialist positioning is the current trend towards downsizing and simplicity for some people in some situations. It creates opportunities for a brand that is universally effective, particularly if it can be flexible while still being simple. An example of this is the Virgin One account, which combines a mortgage, savings and current account in one product.

Having said that, the general trend is still towards specialisation as the means of most effectively creating brand success through meeting consumers' needs. The debate is now less about whether marketing should be aimed at target segments and more about how those segments should be defined. This is the key. The usefulness of segmentation depends heavily on the types of ingredients used, the way they are mixed together, and the extent to which distinct segments actually exist, on any basis.

A General Approach to Segmentation

Single Choice Versus Occasion-driven Markets

This distinction is of primary importance in how you approach segmentation. In some markets, such as toothpaste or washing-up liquid, consumers make a single choice. They have one set of needs from the market, they choose a main brand accordingly, and buy other brands as occasional substitutes. These are essentially single choice markets, where each consumer has one set of needs.

Other markets, such as 'yellow fats' (butter/margarine) or 'eating out venues' are 'occasion-driven' markets. An individual consumer chooses different brands for different types of occasion, having different needs for each of those occasions. In the yellow fats category, the same person may have a repertoire covering:

- a full-fat, high-priced butter for special treats;
- a cheap, basic margarine for cooking; and
- a low-fat, high-quality margarine for normal spreading.

Generally, the decline of the ubiquitous product has meant that many markets are becoming more occasion-driven rather than single choice, and occasions themselves are becoming more flexible and harder to define in simple terms.

Consider beverages as an example. Years ago, tea was the ubiquitous product in the UK. Many people drank almost nothing but tea. They made an overall decision in favour of it, then continued to drink it many times a day out of habit, covering situations where the needs were almost contradictory. They would drink it to wake themselves up in the morning, and to settle themselves down in the evening, ready for sleep. Even today, on average, tea accounts for more than half the liquid consumed by someone aged over 60 in the UK.

Among younger people tea now fits into a much wider repertoire. Broadly speaking, they have a wide set of needs and choose what they want to drink according to how they feel on each occasion, still allowing habit to play a part within each situation.

A friend of mine, when asked to describe his drinking patterns, once said, 'Coffee in the morning, tea in the afternoon, beer in the evening'. This was a simplification, as well as a rather dehydrating menu, though the spirit of the statement was true. The repertoire was essentially defined by familiar behaviour patterns, so the types of occasion could usefully be classified by time of day.

But generally this is now too simple a way of looking at things. We need to define types of occasion more subtly, based more on the different types of needs people have in each situation. For example, in the drinking-out market, we talk about the 'big night out'. It does have some simple day and time emphases, in this case mainly Friday and Saturday evenings, but it is defined primarily by the types of needs people have in such situations.

So this is the trend, and we can anticipate many other categories going in the same direction. Toothpaste and washing-up liquid may be single choice categories today, but we can imagine in the future that they may become occasion-driven. Perhaps many of us will in future use different toothpastes according to the types of food we have been eating during the day.

A General Framework

Traditionally the segmentation task is to put together segments of like-minded people who share the same social values, lifestyles, attitudes to the category and specific needs from the product. Their similarity then means the same set of brands or products should be appropriate for them. Understanding them is the key to:

- identifying which brands or products *should* be appropriate, in terms of specification and marketing communication;
- and then checking whether they are actually choosing the brands or products they 'ought' to be. If not, then it represents an opportunity either to create something new or to move an existing brand towards them.

This general strategy is obviously too crude for occasion-driven markets. There will be no way of putting people into groups, using *any* criteria, that can explain their choices sufficiently well in each situation. It means that any general segmentation approach must incorporate the needs in different situations. So, as a general model, we would say that market segmentation should be viewed in terms of three interlocking issues:

- *why*: the needs fulfilled by brands in that market, overall or in different types of situation;
- *how*: the relationship of the individual to the market (involvement and price); and
- *who*: the type of person (lifestyle, personal values, etc.).

First, on the 'why' level, this works on the logic that brands in a market will be successful if they can tap into a certain need, for example the need to feel important or special. In occasion-driven markets we may identify a type of occasion where people generally have that need.

Then, on the 'how' level, two people may both respond to that need (in that type of occasion), but the product or brand they each buy will differ, according to their relationship with the market, such as how much they are able to pay or are prepared to pay.

Finally, on the 'who' level, different types of people have different ways of expressing or fulfilling a need. So, more outer-directed people will fulfil a need for feeling special with more visible signs than inner-directed people. This may mean you need a different marketing strategy for two different types of people, even though they share the same need and have the same relationship with the category.

A general segmentation framework may look like the one in Figure 5.1. Each segment includes a definition based on the needs, which has implications for the benefits provided by the brand, and it includes a definition based on the person, which will affect the way you communicate with them and present the product or service.

As an example, think of a bar in a town centre. It might be aiming to catch the occasion type of the big night out, in which people have a lot of needs based on excitement, high energy, the stimulation of meeting new people, and so on.

That covers the essential needs, but then there is a choice of style positioning according to the type of person they wish to attract. They may aim for an ultra-trendy style, geared to people who see themselves as trend-setting leaders; or they may aim for a broader, more all-inclusive style, with more mass appeal. Finally, there is a choice of price positioning. Do they want to be exclusively high-priced, or aggressively price-competitive?

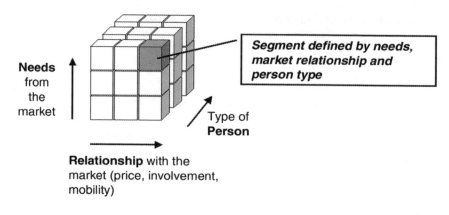

Figure 5.1 General framework for segmentation

Having set up this general framework, it must be admitted that it is rarely followed in practice. Market research more often provides marketing with segmentations based on one or two of these issues, but rarely on all three (needs, market relationship, type of person).

The barrier to using all three types of issue is the complexity. Even if we only create three segments for needs, three for market relationship and three for person type, then we would create 27 segments in total. This is usually too detailed. Most categories do not support brands targeted at segments of less than 5 per cent of the total spending available. However, we often find that there is some correlation between the needs, the market relationship and the person type, as will be seen in the examples below. This means we can collapse the general framework into something simpler.

Before suggesting how best this may be done, we review each of the three areas in turn.

Types of Segmentation

Needs Segmentation ('Why')

A hypothetical example of a needs segmentation for the coffee market is illustrated in Figure 5.2.

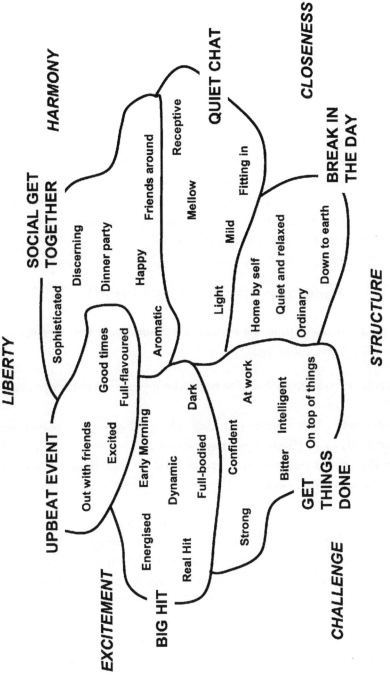

Figure 5.2 Example of needs segmentation

The figure suggests six market segments: social get-together, quiet chat, break in the day, get things done, big hit, and upbeat event. Each segment covers a group of needs, e.g. for *Get Things Done*, the group covers a strong or bitter product, appropriate for work, making the person feel 'on top of it', and expressing a confident or intelligent personality. In terms of the big needs dimensions this segment clearly emphasises 'challenge' and 'structure': the application of assertive energy (challenge) in a practical framework (structure).

The labels for each segment show that we are dealing with an occasion-driven category. The same person will participate in each of the different occasion types, but probably to differing extents. My own coffee drinking happens to be mainly geared to 'getting things done', but there is also some consumption in each of the other segments.

Market Relationship Segmentation ('How')

Setting aside the needs from the market, the main dimensions that matter in the market relationship are:

- **Price**: how much you are able to pay or are prepared to pay for products in this market;
- **Involvement**: how much you care about choice and participate emotionally or in physical purchase volume;
- **Mobility**: how much you are experimental in your brand choice, or open to switching brands.

Price and attitudinal involvement often act together as one broad dimension. High involvement tends to go with a willingness to pay for more expensive brands and not choose simply on the basis of low price. An attitude of low involvement means you are likely to believe that low price brands are good enough to do the job. You don't believe in any of the benefits offered by the high price brands.

Which of the two aspects should be emphasised depends to a large extent on the absolute prices and range of prices in the market. For example, cars are large, expensive purchases, with a huge variation in prices for different models. In this case price is a dominant issue in explaining product choice, and would be the first thing to include. By contrast, toothpaste is a cheap purchase with a relatively narrow price range, and market involvement is more relevant than price.

Mobility, or the desire to experiment, is often somewhat separate from price and involvement. Some people experiment with different brands because they are very price-sensitive; others do so because they are very involved and curious about new products. From the marketer's point of view this connects with behavioural brand loyalty, so they are conscious that 'mobile' people are easy to attract with new products but hard to keep. The new wave of financial services brands in the UK attracted many experimental people, who are more demanding and so were hard to keep when some of those brands failed to maintain the same level of benefits as the competition.

In segmentations based on these sorts of factors, you often find a group of highly involved experimentalists, generally called early adopters. In the launch of any new product, you know it is these people who are likely to be the first to try the product, but that they will frequently drop it later on. The ultimate, settled destination for the new brand will be another segment.

It is often the case that an experimental attitude is most prevalent among younger people, for example in beer drinking. This leads to marketing departments focusing their attention on younger people, to try to convert them to their brand before they become set in their ways. However, there are exceptions such as financial services, where experimentation is likely to go with a degree of confidence in the subject, which is built up through experience over many years.

In fact, it seems likely that experimentation is better explained by an individual's volume of participation in the category than by their age. Young people drink more beer than older people, whereas most older people have more money than younger people. This behavioural factor in involvement is important to consider in segmentation. There is a big prize for converting a heavy category buyer, even if his attitudes are fairly rigid and he is hard to convert. The marketing effort should be worthwhile if he switches to your brand.

A related, more contentious development is the increase in marketing aimed directly at children. Younger children are increasingly becoming a viable target, as they grow up earlier and become more and more influential in brand choice. They have an enthusiasm for consuming information and communication, and are open to discovery. They consume more marketing messages than older people and are very aware of marketing strategies. This very openness and vulnerability is a great concern, and many countries have introduced laws to exert control over marketing at children.

Even if some of these market relationship dimensions are not used to drive a segmentation, it is important to examine them carefully when profiling a segment. That is to say, you may define a segment based on their needs from the category, but you should then look at their market relationship to see the volume the segment accounts for, their propensity to switch brands, and their attitude to price. These things will strongly affect their capacity to be influenced by marketing and the size of the prize for doing so.

People Type Segmentation ('Who')

There would seem to be a huge number of possible characteristics that might be used as a basis for segmenting human beings into groups. A broad potential list might include:

- demographics (e.g. age, gender, life stage, social grade, income);
- lifestyle (e.g. party-goer, workaholic, fitness fanatic, etc.);
- personality (e.g. confident, sociable, quiet, timid);
- social values (e.g. outer-directed vs inner directed, progressive vs conservative).

The first thing to consider is a note of caution. Nowadays people are becoming less easily classifiable into clear groups. There used to be a time when people in the UK of a certain social class and age shared common values, lifestyles and brand choices, but this is becoming less true. And even when we do classify people into such groups, their choice of brands is harder to predict since it increasingly depends on their personal relationship to the category. It means that sophisticated tastes, for example, are less and less a function of social status, and that someone who has a sophisticated attitude to one category, say appreciating good wine, may have a crude approach to another similar category, say their taste in beer. So, segmentation by the type of person works best as a *supporting* tool for a successful marketing strategy, not as the main basis.

Note also that, apart from demographics, the other people descriptors are not stable concepts. People classified as 'party-goers' do not spend every minute of every day at a party. Sociable people are sometimes quiet. Progressive-minded people are occasionally conservative. The picture is much more nebulous, with all of us having all of these characteristics to varying degrees at different times; so this is another reason why people segmentations should be used with caution, and tend to discriminate brand choice rather poorly.

Among the various possibilities, the approach of social values seems to be the most incisive. They all tend to follow the same sort of framework, which we discussed in the first chapter. Here we have added a typical segmentation, illustrated in Figure 5.3.

Our chart shows a possible classification into seven segments, 'adventurer', 'pleasurist' and so on, but there is nothing special about these seven and it may be done in many different ways.

Clearly there is *some* connection between the social values map and the other people issues of demographics, lifestyle and personality. The adventurers will mainly be younger, with an active lifestyle and an outgoing personality, though this is only a tendency, not a close fit. The emphasis on social values is useful because it seems to connect most powerfully with the best way to communicate with segments of people.

Fitting the Issues Together: Needs, Market Relationship, Social Values

So, having described typical segmentations by needs, market relationship and social values, how may they best be fitted together into a single, simpler system that helps effective marketing strategy? Or, put another way, which

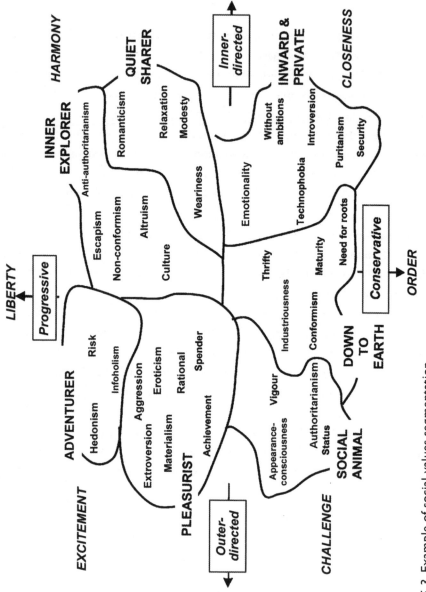

Figure 5.3 Example of social values segmentation

approach is more useful if you cannot include them all without it making things too complicated? We usually find that the three areas are related, rather than being completely independent, so this is a complex question.

First, we often find that a person's needs from a market connect with their overall attitude to participating in that market, so the 'market relationship' information is a supplement to the pure needs-based map.

The involvement and price dimensions tend to connect very broadly with the primary dimension on the needs map, from upper-left to lower-right. If you have a low involvement, you tend to have a simple approach to the category, and are likely to purchase basic, cheap products, that are familiar, easy choices. The mobility dimension frequently goes in the same direction, but is perhaps more vertical: at the top open to new products, at the bottom preferring the tried and tested.

Including the market relationship dimensions directly may help to explain price strata in the market and early adoption of new brands, as well as making sure that marketing does not target segments with a low volume in the market. It is, therefore, an add-on to needs rather than an alternative.

An examination of the social values map and the needs map shows the same broad dimensions at work in both cases, namely excitement–closeness, liberty–structure and harmony–challenge. It follows that there is often a connection, albeit a slight one. If we stir it all together into a system with only half a dozen segments, we might well create a segment based on, say, excitement and liberty, visible to some extent in their market needs *and* their social values.

The big question is what emphasis to give to each one. This depends on what you wish to find out. A segmentation based on needs will explain current brand choice very well, but may offer little information on completely new ideas since it is rooted in the current market situation. Conversely, a segmentation based more on social values or lifestyle may point the way to new possibilities, but be of little use in explaining the current market.

The conclusion from the above discussion is that the best marketing strategies are based on needs, but are refined by incorporating social values and market relationship.

Getting the Best out of Segmentation

Enough evidence has been gathered in the market research industry to show that segmentations based just on the type of person (lifestyle, values, etc.) often discriminate brand choice very poorly. This is the case in single choice categories, not just in occasion-driven categories where the individual's repertoire of needs and brands will further reduce any differences. So, we know that the most useful segmentations start with people's needs from the category, split by types of people if this is appropriate. Even then, it raises the question of the value of doing this. Clearly we are recommending that a brand should focus on its brand promise, and connect this with important needs in the market, but it is worth going further.

The whole principle of segmenting implies that the divisions are not just arbitrary cuts in a continuum of attitude. They should reveal segments that are genuinely separate, with big gaps between them. The statistical technique typically used in quantitative studies is called cluster analysis, with the aim of identifying nicely clustered groups. Imagine people sitting on lots of little islands, each person close to the others on the same island, and far away from those sitting on other islands.

This analogy does highlight one important situation. Remember the cold and flu remedy example, where we suggested that the market polarised between 'challenge' (getting on with it, coping, attacking the cold) versus 'harmony' (giving in, being cared for, gentle and soothing remedies that ease the symptoms and restore your balance). Now, I don't know whether this is the exact situation, but it suggests that an analysis of the *average* importance of the needs in the market would be misleading. Aspects such as the power and gentleness of the remedy might appear only moderately important on average, yet they are each crucially important to some people in some situations. If your market is genuinely polarised, then some form of segmentation could be important and revealing.

Let us end on a note of realism. Over the years I have frequently asked brand managers to describe the target for their brand, in terms of needs or people, then in quantitative surveys we obtained data that profiled the users or buyers of that brand, or the reasons for using it. As a very rough rule of thumb, only half of the purchasing falls within the target. It doesn't mean it is wrong to have a target in mind, it just illustrates that in reality you will attract a much wider audience.

Arguably it is more useful to identify a 'bull's-eye' of where your brand is aiming, in terms of the 'who, why, how' structure. When the brand manager thinks of this brand, what sort of person do they have in mind, and why, how and when are they going to use the brand? This is immediately useful in advertising, as well as providing a focus for all marketing and product or service development.

6

Turning Brand
Equity into Sales

All the previous chapters have talked in positive terms about the reasons why people would want to buy a brand – the way it meets important needs, how its equity shows the total benefit it offers, how it presents itself coherently through different touchpoints, and how it might focus successfully on a particular target of types of people or situations. There now remains the challenge of establishing a link between this attitudinal response by consumers and actual sales of a brand. Given that brand equity is the sum of these positive attitudes, the key is to explore the relationship between equity and sales and see what else, if anything, is required to make the connection.

In some categories you see a very close correlation between brand equity and brand sales, but more typically you see quite large variations. There are a number of reasons for this, which can be grouped under the headings of 'pull' and 'push'.

Brand Pull

Brand pull covers people's attitudes to brands and categories. It covers all the factors that indicate someone's likelihood to buy a brand, once it has been made available and drawn to their attention. Apart from brand equity, the other influential factors are price/value, involvement and mobility. Each of these is discussed below.

Price and Value

Understanding and measuring the workings of price is a vast subject, and here we draw attention to only a couple of aspects.

First, it should be appreciated that price is simply a choice of brand position in a market. There is no *general* relationship between a brand's relative price and its market share. In some categories the premium price brands are successful, while in others the lower priced brands are successful. This is illustrated in Figure 6.1, which was compiled using research and development work by Ipsos.

The important concept is value for money, meaning the combination between price and the desire to buy the brand. It doesn't matter what price you charge, so long as it is appropriate for what you are offering, represented by the brand equity.

Value is the important concept, but it is not very insightful to ask people to give a direct rating of the value for money of a brand. A better approach, certainly one that produces a better explanation of their behaviour, is to ask their perceptions of price (not value) or to use actual market price. Then we compare this to each brand's equity and obtain a measure of value for money.

To do this well you need to allow for the varying importance of price in different categories, and to take into account how price is presented and interpreted. In some cases price is very visible and straightforward (e.g. consumer packaged goods). In other categories, such as financial services, it is important but more complicated. The way a consumer identifies and determines the price of a service, or the return on an investment, may not be consistent or logical. There are also some areas where price plays no part at all, such as choice between terrestrial television channels or radio channels, though the major themes within brand equity do still apply.

Of course, this line of analysis assumes that price and equity are independent of each other. It carries the logic that if you reduce your price so your product becomes more 'desirable', then your equity will stay the same but your brand's value for money will become stronger. This may well be true for small price movements, but care is needed. In many cases people

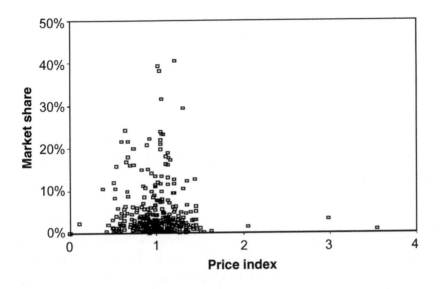

Figure 6.1 Market share vs relative price.
Reproduced with kind permission from IPSOS.

infer a level of quality according to the price they are charged. Occasionally you find a category where quality is objectively visible, although this is rare. More often it is a combination of some objective judgement and a lot of blind faith, and some brands deliberately play on this fact, for example Stella Artois with its slogan 'reassuringly expensive'.

The measure of value for money is not necessarily a simple equation between equity and price across a whole category. Towards the upper end, the premium manufacturers' brands need to lean heavily on all aspects of equity, in order to justify their price. At the lower end, including supermarkets' own labels, it is more a question of the brand simply being 'good enough to do the job'.

Consumers' Involvement

You can identify brands from different categories with equally good equity, price and marketing support, but sometimes you find they achieve different levels of success in the marketplace. The reason for this is often consumers' level of 'involvement' in the category and the brand. At the category level, involvement means the extent of consumer interest in the category: how much they care about their choice of brands. If they do not care very much, it weakens the benefit you can expect from positive attitudes to the brand. They *say* your brand is fantastic, but in the end they may not care enough for that attitude to turn into choice behaviour.

One classic example of this is the batteries category. People have many positive perceptions of the brand Duracell, but that level of positive attitude does not translate into sales as strongly as we find in other categories.

The category attitude is modified by a more specific attitude to each brand. This emerges as a question of substitutability, meaning the question of whether another brand is considered able to do the same job. It operates as a tougher test than simply identifying differences in perceptions between two brands.

You might expect that this issue would be strongly connected to the price position of the brand, but this is not always so. As an example, consider a study of the UK dog food market carried out in the early 1990s. The study revealed the fairly typical characteristic of a closely competing group of medium-low price brands (Bounce, Chappie, Bonus), but also a distinct low price brand (Chappie) that did not overlap with the others at a similar price level. The brand Chappie in the UK had a particular formulation that was recommended by vets for its digestive qualities, so it had a genuine point of difference. (Note that the brand name Chappie is applied to different products in other countries.)

What we should learn from this is that any brand can have an aspect that creates a distinctive point of difference, regardless of its price position in the category.

These things can sometimes change quite quickly. A category can become commoditised, so people believe it is not worth buying 'better' products. In such a case many consumers become bargain hunters, increasingly susceptible to the promotional activity of shops' own labels, thus reducing the amount of purchases they make of the higher-priced brand. If the big brands join in price wars, they increase the likelihood of consumers' losing faith in their quality.

Mobility and Inertia

Generally, consumers have become more confident. They have fewer anxieties about brands and are more confident about switching or simply checking out different brands. There is more choice available, and they have been increasingly encouraged to try different brands. Years ago, if someone had a low level of involvement or care about a category, then they would most likely stick with one familiar brand. Nowadays, a similar low attitude is more likely to mean that they see many brands as potential substitutes for each other, and so have little inclination to stick with one.

Positive involvement in a category, or concern about which brand to choose, used to manifest itself as careful selection of the one brand you felt suited you best. Now, such positive involvement is likely to mean an enthusiasm for trying new brands and a selection of a repertoire of brands to meet different needs on different occasions. High involvement means someone is more likely to choose the better quality or higher priced brands, but it generally does not mean higher behavioural loyalty to a brand. Behavioural loyalty to a brand is declining.

We talk about a dimension of 'mobility' and its opposite, 'inertia'. A mobile consumer is one who is highly mobile between brands. They are inclined to make changes. Even if they are reasonably satisfied with a brand they may wish to check out other brands, either because they enjoy doing so, or to find out if there is a better alternative available. Inertia is the opposite concept, meaning an inclination to stick with a brand, even if you are dissatisfied with it.

Changes taking place in the modern world of brands mean there is more mobility and less inertia. In some cases there has been a practical reduction in the 'pain of change', making it physically easier to move. For example, it has become easier in the UK to switch suppliers of various financial services, such as current accounts and mortgages. The reduction in the pain of change is, for the most part, also a change of mindset as well as physical constraints.

Over recent years the financial services category has seen the arrival of new market entrants offering very good deals, successfully attracting customers. The new customers are, by nature, very mobile and demanding. So, subsequent reductions in the financial value of those products inclined many of those customers to look elsewhere. Mobility works both ways: it is easier to attract mobile customers but also easier to lose them.

The reverse situation is often found for long-established market leading brands, such as Prudential or British Telecom. They are likely to have relatively strong behavioural loyalty, compared to the attitudes to the brand, since they will have many immobile customers – people who can't be bothered to move, even if they are dissatisfied. Over time there is a risk that this may become a problem, as these markets have opened up to greater competition and the arrival of new types of company, which encourages even relatively immobile people to rethink their situation.

Brand Push

All the components we have described up to this point are descriptions of how consumers relate to brands and categories. We have covered:

- the consumer needs met by a brand;
- consumers' perceptions of a brand's equity, and thus a measure of how much they desire the brand;
- the value for money offered by a brand, meaning its equity in relation to its price;
- how these opinions are either translated into choice of the best value brands, or dampened through a lack of care about the category;
- how levels of mobility or inertia in the category will affect the speed with which people act on their feelings, either through their own desires or practical barriers; and
- how these various aspects are influenced through the different touchpoints between the brand and the consumer, particularly the differences between direct experience and reaction to advertising.

Collectively these represent the 'pull' of the brand: how much consumers want it once it's in front of them. The other remaining factors we call brand 'push', meaning how much the company has pushed the product or service to the attention of the consumer. The elements we find within brand push are:

- the *opportunity* to buy it: e.g. the distribution of packaged goods, the accessibility of retailers, the route coverage of airlines;
- *visual prominence*: e.g. the amount of shelf space and pack stand-out of packaged goods brands, the visibility of the shop front and the quality of location for retailers;
- *promotions activity*: drawing extra attention to the brand and giving an extra benefit such as a chance to win or collect free gifts;
- *price discounts and price promotions*: anything where the price paid per unit is less than standard price, including offers such as 'buy one get one free' as well as straightforward price cuts;
- *direct mail* into people's homes; and
- *advertising or sponsorship*, in the specific sense of creating top-of-mind awareness and promoting visual triggers that encourage purchase. Note: this is different from the role of advertising in building brands through eliciting brand pull.

To some extent, marketing can use these push factors independently of brand pull, creating immediate changes in the sales of the brand. Changes in those push levers generally have a short-term impact through that channel, but also tend to influence brand pull over the longer term. For example:

- advertising drives long-term changes in brand attitudes, as well higher short-term sales through raised top-of-mind awareness;
- price position implies a quality expectation, and so a change in price affects attitudes over the longer term, as well as short-term sales;
- many types of promotion are known to reduce consumers' beliefs that the brand is worth paying more for, and so erode positive attitudes over time;
- wide distribution and a strong, visible presence can carry the implication that the brand is popular, successful and therefore worth

buying since lots of other people must be buying it; conversely, a lower availability and visibility can help support a position of exclusivity in certain cases.

The rigid separation of push and pull factors can therefore be slightly misleading, particularly if it is taken to imply that any push factor may be manipulated without long-term consequences for the brand's attitudes, since this is not the case.

Generally, push factors can change quickly, while pull factors will move more slowly. So, short-term sales fluctuations are usually the result of a change in some push factor. There are some exceptions to this, particularly if a brand hits problems in performance quality, but it is a good general rule. Indeed, if you hold the view that any brand attitude 'worth having' will have been built up over a period of time, then you would expect brand pull to be something whose value changes slowly.

Brand pull represents the underlying strength of the brand, once the support elements through brand push have been stripped away. This approach to defining it has considerable merit. It shows in some way what all these consumer attitudes are 'worth' to the brand, since it puts them in a framework whose currency is market share. This does not mean it is easy to measure in this way – far from it; it simply has a place in the scheme of things.

So, brand pull represents the concept of the competitiveness of the brand in its market, assessed on a level playing-field against other brands. It is broadly true that big brands are also strong brands, since they tend to be identified as strong and then given strong marketing support, which in turn makes them bigger and stronger. However, we do see wide variations: for example, two major brands of lager in the UK had roughly the same brand pull, but one had over 25 per cent higher sales, due to much stronger brand push.

This provides an answer to someone challenging the benefit of studying brand attitudes, if they say 'I can see how healthy my brand is from its sales'. The truth is they can guess to some extent, but they can't see to what extent they may be supporting a weak brand, or spot the warning signs when their underlying brand strength starts to erode.

The Outcomes or Benefits of a Strong Brand

What are the benefits of having a strong brand, or more precisely a brand with good equity? Two major themes can be identified, with various aspects within each.

Current strength

- Higher sales than other brands.
- Able to sell at a higher price than other brands.
- Resistance among current customers to competitors' marketing activity.

Future outlook

- Growth in sales of this brand, if your brand is currently small.
- Ongoing high sales, if your brand is already big.
- Cross-selling: likelihood of purchasing new products or services connected with the same brand.

The three benefits resulting from 'current strength' are related, but not completely interchangeable. Markets vary in price sensitivity, so you can find some price-sensitive categories where a strong brand does *not* really have the ability to sell at a price premium. Similarly, categories vary in consumers' level of mobility and responsiveness to marketing activity, hence they vary in the size of the third benefit: resistance to competitors' marketing.

Regarding the second theme of 'future outlook', again you will find differences between categories and brands, although the issues are linked. The current size of your brand will indicate whether there is scope for the brand to grow, or whether the focus should be more on protecting the current level of sales. Cross-selling is also a major issue for some categories but not others, particularly for services categories covering a variety of types of product.

Rather than having six (or more) different measures of brand strength, it is more useful to reduce them to one or two, particularly for the purpose of comparing across categories. The items within the theme of current strength can be combined, as can those within the future outlook, but the two big themes cannot be combined into one score. This might be likened to concepts in physics of position and trajectory, which are clearly quite separate. In fact, they often contrast (see Figure 6.2). Many brands with high current strength are likely to go down in the future, while many brands with low current strength are well placed to go up.

Is it better to be small and growing, or big and stable? The answer depends on your time horizon. If you are taking a long-term view, you will place more weight on the future outlook, whereas if you are concerned with the short term you will be more interested in current strength.

Given that the current strength and future outlook often contradict, it is no surprise that the attitudinal indicators of each are quite different. Market researchers usually create a measure of current strength by adding up all the good things consumers say about a brand. They may use specific brand perceptions, or equity components, or sometimes more global questions such as asking brand preference.

One specific variation is to focus just on the outcome of the brand's ability to charge a higher price, and to measure this through a piece of research about pricing. This method is clear in its intentions, but may be more or less appropriate according to the importance of that outcome in the category you are studying.

A future outlook score is more likely to be determined from looking at the *balance* between different equity components, rather than their absolute scores. For example, is a brand's relevance higher than its level of familiarity? The patterns you find through this approach are often complex, and can easily be thrown off course by the intrusion of other factors, such as changes of marketing plans. This subject is covered more fully in Chapter 7.

Behavioural Brand Loyalty

There seems to be two ways of having high sales. You can either have many people who buy your brand, or you can have fewer buyers who buy your brand a lot. Using marketing terminology, the first approach focuses on the

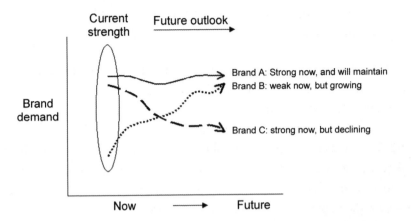

Figure 6.2 Current strength and future outlook

penetration of buyers, while the second focuses on the *behavioural loyalty* to the brand.

These two strategies have been hotly debated over recent years. The reason for this is that behavioural loyalty has been found to be generally higher for brands with a high penetration of buyers. This phenomenon is called 'double jeopardy'. It states that not only do big brands have more people buying them than buy smaller brands, but those people are also more behaviourally loyal. Big brands have the 'double benefit' of more buyers *and* more behavioural loyalty among those buyers.

In fact, this is not just broadly true, it is almost unavoidable for some mathematical reasons, which can be demonstrated by the following simple example. Imagine a small island with a population of 100 people (see Figure 6.3). Everyone buys a particular product category, and it is a very simple category with only two brands available, labelled A and B. Brand A is the bigger of the two, with 80 buyers. Brand B is smaller, with only 40 buyers. When you think about it, this must mean that there are 20 people who buy both brands. If you add the 80 buyers of Brand A to the 40 buyers of Brand B then you get 120, which must mean there are 20 who buy both.

To keep things straightforward, let's look at a simple measure of brand loyalty, in this case 'the proportion of buyers of the brand who *only* buy that brand'. We find that:

- the loyalty for Brand A is 60 divided by 80, i.e. 75 per cent;
- the loyalty for Brand B is 20 divided by 40, i.e. 50 per cent.

So three out of four buyers of Brand A are loyal to it, whereas the same is true for only half of the buyers of Brand B.

The key point about this example is that the bigger brand, i.e. the one with more buyers, *automatically* has more loyal customers than the smaller brand. It is mathematically inevitable. Obviously, in a more complicated market we do see slight divergences, but the general pattern tends to remain substantially true. The double jeopardy effect means that big brands achieve a disproportionately high market share.

Figure 6.4 (opposite) shows a real example illustrating this point. It shows the relationship between penetration of buyers and market share for a specific category.

To understand how this graph relates to brand loyalty, first you must appreciate that market share is a function of brand penetration and loyalty, if we define them in the following ways:

- brand penetration=how many people buy the brand;
- brand loyalty=how often those people buy that brand rather than another brand;
- therefore, brand penetration × brand loyalty=the total purchases of the brand, which is its market share.

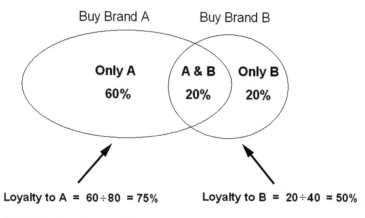

Figure 6.3 Behavioural brand loyalty

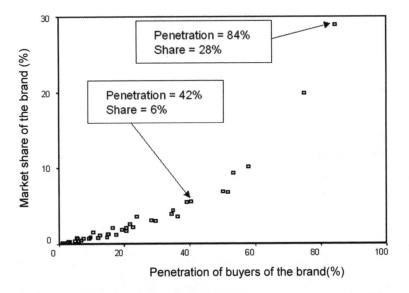

Figure 6.4 Market share vs brand penetration.
Reproduced with kind permission from IPSOS.

The key to interpreting Figure 6.4 is brand loyalty, which explains the link between penetration of buyers (on the horizontal axis) and market share (on the vertical axis). Here you can clearly see that the pattern is a curve, not a straight line. The brand with 84 per cent penetration of buyers has much more than double the market share of the brand with 42 per cent penetration. An immediate consequence is that it is of no importance to find that a bigger brand has higher behavioural loyalty than a smaller brand. It is *not* an interesting finding! It only becomes interesting if you compare the actual loyalty of a brand against the level you would expect for a brand of that size. Nine times out of ten this will show a negligible difference between the actual result and the expected result. Only occasionally will it reveal anything worthy of attention.

As well as the mathematical reasons, you can hypothesise many marketing reasons why this might be the case. For example, a brand with high loyalty will have many satisfied customers, they will tell other people about their experiences, and some of those people will try the brand. Conversely, lower behavioural loyalty is typically an indication that many current buyers do not appreciate the brand sufficiently, so some of them will drop it.

Some brands are in a strong niche and have a disproportionately high loyalty, but usually a competitor arrives to change this – don't expect to buck the trend for long.

The general point of learning for marketing strategy is: do not try to build a marketing plan based deliberately on high loyalty and few buyers, or even the reverse, on low loyalty but lots of buyers. It may work in the short term, but the mathematical evidence is that in the longer term, it will settle into the predictable pattern.

7

Ups and Downs:
Today is Fine,
How About Tomorrow?

Forces that Drive Brands Up or Down

In Chapter 6 we drew a distinction between the study of a brand's current strength and its outlook for the future. Indeed, the biggest challenges in the study of brands are forecasting the future and distinguishing cause and effect. These are obviously related, since the ability to predict depends on our skill in identifying causes of change. Many of these causes are factors outside the control of the company and cannot easily be anticipated, such as changes in legislation, social trends, unexpected world events, the arrival of a new competitor, or even a change of brand manager or brand strategy.

Some of these things have a major effect on a category as a whole, for example social trends and seasonal variations, and so it is easier to study changes in a brand's market share rather than its absolute sales. But even then, there are many examples of big success stories where one brand in a category has seized a trend opportunity ahead of its rivals. So concentrating on forecasting market share only slightly decreases the difficulties.

Furthermore, the various factors often have a compound effect that is greater than the sum of the parts. When things are going well for your brand, you find one good thing reinforces another. Conversely, when things are going badly, it is hard to reverse a downward trend. On top of all this, the situation is obviously very different according to the current size of your brand. Big brands have little space to go up, but a long way to fall, while the reverse is true for small brands. Any analysis also has to take this sort of factor into account.

One choice is whether to include different scenarios for changes in the 'push' factors, in our anticipation of the future success of the brand. If this is done, then it allows scope for more refined marketing models. However, in this chapter, we will focus on brand 'pull', looking to understand the consumer factors that reveal a brand's future outlook, with the proviso 'other things being equal'.

Despite the difficulties involved, quite a lot is now known about the patterns that tend to indicate the likely growth or decline of a brand. Many independent market research studies have been done to try to spot the consumer brand attitude factors that anticipate brand growth and decline. This is taking brand equity and loyalty, and focusing on its benefit for the future of the brand, rather than the explanation of current brand strength. Less work has been done so far on integrating this with all the relevant factors to provide a complete picture.

We have grouped the various issues into three types:

- the market context;
- the brand's marketing and consumer response;
- social trends.

The first of these relates to the context in which your marketing has to operate. It includes the understanding of consumer behaviour, mathematical laws about brand growth and decline, and the typical situation for your brand in terms of history and marketing budget. Next we look at the different types of marketing approach that can be adopted, including the focus on different equity components, and lessons learned about modern marketing. Finally we examine social trends, on the basis that any brand that can catch an important trend will have a future advantage over those that do not.

The application of the marketing context and a brand's own marketing differs to a large extent between big brands and small brands. Big brands tend to be in a defensive position, concerned to maintain their size and avoid going down. Conversely, small brands are often in more of an attacking position, needing to go up in order to survive. The key characteristics in each case are summarised in Figures 7.1 and 7.2, which cover big brands and small brands respectively.

The Market Context

Mathematical Factors

Setting aside all issues of marketing, there are some mathematical laws which potentially influence the progress of brands.

On the one hand there is the question of double jeopardy, where big brands have greater behavioural loyalty from their customers as well as simply having a larger number of customers. Given that behaviour reinforces attitudes, this will therefore help push up the big brands and hold down the little brands. Balanced against this is the concept of the amount of 'space' for change. There is simply more room for big brands to go down and for small brands to go up. Mathematicians will be familiar with this concept as 'regression to the mean'.

Overall these two forces seem to cancel each other out. The bigger brand is held up by its loyalty but has further to fall. The smaller brand has weaker loyalty but more room to go up. So this leads to the conclusion that if your behavioural loyalty is above par for your brand size, then you are in a strong position, but if it is below what you should expect for your brand size then you are vulnerable.

Market Factors

This covers the gradual changes in markets and marketing, as well as some questions of the 'marketing muscle' for different brands. They work in less consistent ways than the mathematical forces, in some cases jeopardising both large and small brands, and in other cases favouring one over the other.

Go down

Go up/Stay up

Mathematically more 'space' to go down

Double jeopardy: greater loyalty and customer base

Proliferation of companies
Specialisation
Fast-changing world
Any brand can 'do the job'

Bigger budgets for marketing
More clout on push factors
Benefit of heritage

Mass market brand vulnerable to cheaper imitators
Skin deep differentiation
Missing a trend, losing relevance
Changing too much, loss of identity and understanding

Reinventing yourself, catching a trend
Insulation from competition, differences that are hard to copy

Market context

Your own marketing

Figure 7.1 Reasons for big(ger) brands to go up or down

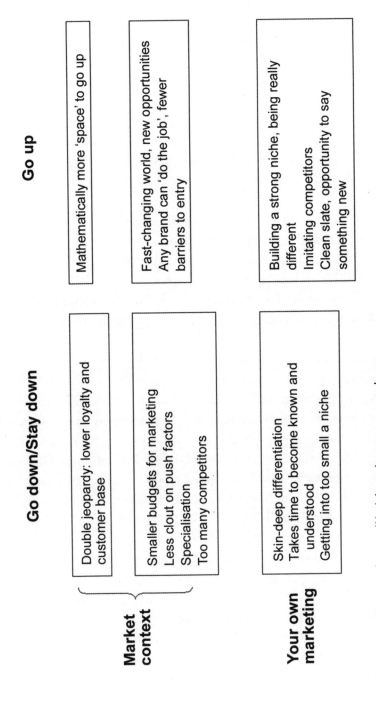

Go down/Stay down

Go up

Double jeopardy: lower loyalty and customer base

Mathematically more 'space' to go up

Smaller budgets for marketing
Less clout on push factors
Specialisation
Too many competitors

Fast-changing world, new opportunities
Any brand can 'do the job', fewer barriers to entry

Market context

Skin-deep differentiation
Takes time to become known and understood
Getting into too small a niche

Building a strong niche, being really different
Imitating competitors
Clean slate, opportunity to say something new

Your own marketing

Figure 7.2 Reasons for small(er) brands to go up or down

Increased competition and the tendency towards specialisation make it harder for *any* brand to become large or to stay large. There is nearly always a new competitor arriving on the scene, strongly adapted to meet the specific needs targeted by your brand. Some markets may have reached saturation, but in general this is a challenge for existing brands.

By contrast, the fast pace of change in the modern world and the growing perception that any brand can 'do the job' are factors that help new entrants into a market. Consumers are increasingly open to trying new brands and believing that they will perform well, so this can help the prospects of small brands, but poses a threat to larger brands.

Balanced against this is the muscle of the larger brand. Typically bigger brands are supported by bigger marketing budgets, they can draw on the strength of their heritage, and they have more clout on the push factors in terms of distribution and point of sale impact.

Overall, the market factors therefore seem fairly balanced. Individual cases will be positive or negative according to the marketing muscle behind a particular brand, large or small.

There are, however, other factors that affect the fortunes of all the brands in a category, except those competing on lower price. The growing confidence in the functional effectiveness of all brands, the explosion of choice, promotions and price wars, has 'commoditised' many categories. You reach a stage where people do not believe it is worth paying more for a branded product, so they start to choose on the basis of price. They either make a consistent choice of a low-price product, or they become bargain hunters, prepared to switch brands to get the best deal. This obviously hurts every brand, big and small.

Closely allied to this is the level of involvement of consumers in the category – how much they care about their choices between brands. We pointed out earlier that brands operating in high involvement categories achieve better sales than those with similar good attitudes in low involvement categories. People act on their positive attitudes to a brand when involvement is high, but do this less when involvement is low – they perceive that your brand has advantages over others, but don't care enough to act on those perceptions. This means that low involvement has a dampening effect on the progress of brands. Changes of attitudes to a brand are less likely to lead to a change in consumer behaviour.

In the same vein, some categories display greater responsiveness to advertising than other categories, and indeed there will be differences between brands within a category. This is very similar to the way in which there are category differences in price elasticity, and differences between brands in a category. Equally, some categories are clearly structured and organised according to the benefits provided by brands, such as butter and margarine, while other categories are more confused, such as toothbrushes. This context makes it easier or harder for product differentiation to be understood by the consumer.

In summary, categories vary in their responsiveness to each marketing lever (advertising, price, product, etc.) and there are differences between the brands in each category. These factors all affect the ease or difficulty of moving a brand.

The Brand's Marketing and Consumer Response

The Marketing and Consumer Response for Larger Brands

Here the picture is more varied, and is more to do with the particular strategy of a brand and how effectively it is pursued. The lessons seem to be somewhat different for large and small brands. On the positive side, larger brands do well if they can constantly reinvent themselves, being prepared to latch onto new trends or more generally to move with the times. A strong example of such a move was made by Marks & Spencer in the UK after the Second World War. It spotted the opportunity to catch the new wave of growing middle class aspiration to quality, and moved the brand upwards out of the low price segment. The history of M&S has been a story of sometimes catching and leading new trends, and at other times missing a trend or losing touch with its customers' needs.

Another key issue for a large brand is its ability to maintain strong differentiation. They are automatically relevant to a wide audience, otherwise they wouldn't be big, but the challenge is then to be genuinely distinctive rather than 'all things to all people'. This becomes critical when the differentiation is strong enough to mean insulation from competition, based on differences which are hard to copy.

Some of the dangers for a large brand reflect the positive aspects. Skin-deep differentiation will mean the brand is not well insulated from competition and can easily be substituted by other brands. And if brands are too rigid, they may miss a trend and lose relevance, because the market has moved on and consumers' needs have changed. However successful they have been in the past, big brands must continue to innovate. But there is an attendant risk if a well-known brand tries to change too much, or in ways that are not credible, leading to a loss of clarity about the identity of the brand.

Other specific problems may arise if the brand is competing in the mass market, rather than at a premium price. In this case it is vulnerable to cheaper imitators, especially if it is perceived to be easily substitutable. In this case a higher price offers some defence against low price competition, assuming it is accompanied by the necessary quality. We see plenty of examples of mainstream brands in vigorous price competition with each other, with low behavioural loyalty and high perceived substitutability. Such brands have little opportunity to grow and are constantly vulnerable to attack.

Marketing and Consumer Response for Smaller Brands

Marketing strategy for new brands or small brands is inevitably different to that for larger brands. A first important principle is the need to establish an identity, growing familiarity or understanding of the brand. On the whole, people will not buy something they are not clear about. Familiarity is not sufficient in itself to guarantee success, but it does seem to act as a necessary precondition. Note that this is different from simple awareness of the brand; it is more about getting across a clear message to the consumer.

Beyond that, small brands have a variety of opportunities. They can aim to be really different and build a strong niche. In the longer term this will become limiting, and then the combination of differentiation and relevance will be important. Alternatively, they can adopt a predatory approach, deliberately aiming to copy other brands.

In terms of differentiation they face the same challenges as larger brands. It must be more than skin-deep. This may present a challenge, since it can take time to become known and for people to develop a depth of knowledge about the brand that supports the view that it offers something genuinely different.

Once some familiarity or understanding of the brand has been established, and a clear point of difference been communicated to attract attention, the critical factor is then the relevance of the brand to a large audience. Very often, through a desire to say something different, a new brand will face the problem that it has communicated a narrow positioning. This means there is a low ceiling on the number of people who considered the brand relevant to them, i.e. there is some factor that makes many people feel the brand cannot meet their needs or lifestyle.

A Summary of General Patterns

The above discussion makes it clear that the situation is complex, and that it is hard to draw simple, general conclusions. Indeed, there is a danger of oversimplification. Having said that, we can draw out some general themes.

Relative comparisons: In terms of brand equity components, it is generally the balance between the different indicators that is more important than the absolute levels of the indicators. For example, high relevance in itself is not good or bad for the future outlook of the brand, but how this compares with the other items is important.

The engine room: We can reasonably think of an 'engine room' for a brand, based on a combination of its differentiation, its relevance and sometimes its quality. If this is strong compared to the other pillars of equity, then the brand generally has good potential for growth, while if the engine is weak the brand is vulnerable.

Familiarity or understanding the brand: This is double-edged. When building a small brand, you have to get this across. The engine is no good if people haven't understood the message that it's there and what it's about. However, high familiarity is a negative unless the engine is equally strong.

Insulation and market structure: All the above is affected by the nature of the category and your place within it. Your brand can be insulated through exclusive price or a niche with few real competitors able to do the same job. In particular, this can protect you from attack by predatory lower-priced brands.

The right amount of differentiation: There is an art in finding the right balance. The big, most successful brands are able to find a reasonable level of differentiation without narrowing their appeal and losing relevance.

The power of popularity: Brand equity components such as 'popularity', 'esteem' or 'prominence' are sometimes viewed as almost negative by-products of success, indicators of likely decline if they are not matched by the strength of the engine room for a brand. Yet in some cases they help *sustain* a dominant position in the market.

Old Marketing and New Marketing

Throughout this book we have commented on the changes in the dynamics of market structure, consumer needs and the way people view brands. These are reflected by changes in the way marketing is approached today compared to in the past.

Flexibility: One key theme is flexibility in the ways brands are marketed, corresponding with growing flexibility in market structures and the ways consumers make choices. There is a move towards creating brands based on ideas or principles in a flexible way that allows them to enter different categories and to keep up with the fast pace of change in modern society. Another facet of this is our growing desire to be in control and to customise brands to our own requirements, so many brands are now marketed with deliberate flexibility in mind.

Closeness to individuals: Brands are now marketed to build closer relationships with customers. In the past there was a relationship, but it was based more on aspirational values for brands, and so it maintained a distance between the brand and the person. Now, it is more a relationship of equals, fuelled by a much greater variety of marketing channels that can be used, as well as the growth of databases of information about individual customers, which allows the brand to speak more directly and personally to each individual.

Different or better: Fifty years ago a brand was marketed to be 'different because it was better', in terms of its functional or aspirational quality. Now people are less impressed by claims of a brand's superiority, and brands are increasingly marketed to be 'better because it is different' – a question of a brand suiting your personal style, preferences or way of life.

Social Trends

Many of the changes in our society can be well described by simple demographics. For example, in the UK, health improvements mean people live longer, and the tendency is towards smaller families, started later in life. And when you add economic changes to this picture, you can explain quite a lot of the changing fortunes of various types of product.

Beyond that, there are many more subtle social trends. An excellent presentation of trends and opportunities for brands is made by John Grant in his book *The New Marketing Manifesto*. Taking the subject wider, Figure 7.3 looks at some of the trends in society associated with each of the fundamental needs.

Small Planet and the Spiritual Search (Ideals)

An obvious, and much talked about, trend is the one we have called 'small planet', linked to the need for ideals. It covers globalisation, both the increased commonality of brand experience across countries and the changes in people's sense of identity. This now crosses boundaries more readily, fostering new notions of community and a more global

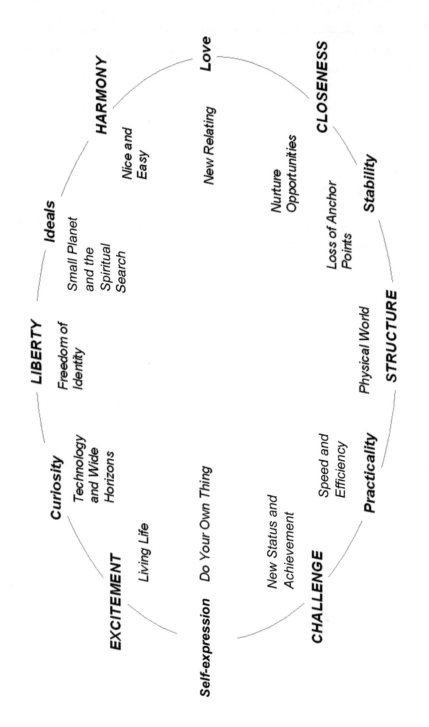

Figure 7.3 Social trends

responsibility. The 'citizen of the world' connection is a growing potential hook for many brands, e.g. 'United Colors of Benetton'.

A big part of this is the notion of fairness, and how the frame of reference for this is expanding. It means fairness that cuts across traditional boundaries such as family, local community, peer group or country. In this context today we see a wave of global brands being held much more to account for their actions and their social responsibility. This can happen to any global brand, regardless of its positioning according to human needs, but the attention is increased if a brand deliberately tries to tap into this need for ideals. There is a growing public awareness of what organisations perceive to be the reality in different countries for different people, through the dramatic increases in travel and media coverage.

On a more personal level, there have never been so many opportunities for self-improvement or inner exploration through hobbies, self-education and the like, and these are increasingly open to everyone rather than being the province of a few. At the same time, we seem to have entered a second wave of New Age holistic perspective on the world, a more private exploration of our values, perhaps supported by science but not derived from science.

Nice and Easy (Harmony)

The world is loosening up, in terms of an easier informality in the way we deal with each other. Not so long ago formal clothes were standard wear in an office. Then came the introduction of 'dress-down Friday'. Now in those same places you find the code is 'dress down on Mondays to Thursdays and dress as roughly as possible on Friday'.

The recognition of authority and social status is gone. It feels uncomfortable to be addressed as 'sir' or 'madam', where once you might have been offended if these terms were not used in certain situations. This extends to a discomfort with formal, inflexible procedures in our dealings with brands. Form-filling, red tape and bureaucracy is very out of date. We now expect flexibility of alternatives and ease in making things happen.

This has implications for many brands, particularly service brands, in the way they present themselves to customers, regardless of whether they particularly try to tap this need, and there are clearly opportunities for those that do aim for it. The brand easyJet is an obvious example of a brand that taps this trend towards informality.

At the same time we lead such hectic lives that the need for calm is emphasised, the more we are denied it by the pace of life. Anything which reduces the white noise and information overload is therefore a growing opportunity. You might include brands such as the Virgin One account here, that simplify your financial arrangements so that life is easier, but without disadvantaging you financially.

New Relating (Love)

There seem to be many changes in the world of relationships. There is the move away from the structure of fixed family, relatives and neighbours, towards a wider circle of people who define our lives. There are greater technological facilities for communication, all of which actually serve to emphasise the need for personal human contact. The way we meet people and relate to them is constantly changing.

Obviously telecommunications companies are now all alert to these changes, particularly having experienced the unpredicted growth of text messaging. And of course there will be many other opportunities for different types of service that facilitate communication between people, such as Internet chatrooms and a widening range of dating agencies and common interest groups. It also implies a change in the way packaged goods brands can move away from very traditional images of the family circle towards a wider frame of reference.

Nurture Opportunities (Closeness)

Many of the changes we are describing give a new resonance to a need, as it becomes denied through traditional channels. One of these is the need to nurture and create a caring environment. Postponing having children, or indeed deciding not to have children at all, means these needs will come out in different ways. We commented earlier on the increase in brands connected with nurturing activities such as gardening and home decoration. This would seem to be at least partly fuelled by the 'nurture' desire having to find new outlets. An offshoot of this trend is 'homes from home', where we see home-like environments set up in offices and coffee shops.

The flip-side of the desire to nurture is the need to feel nurtured. The world feels a very unpredictable, open place now that the horizons have been opened up. The nostalgia ticket is a great opportunity for making people feel safe, reminding them of a time when they were nurtured. It means 'the way mother used to make it', and that feeling of being a child again.

Loss of Anchor Points (Stability)

We don't live in an amoral society, but our sense of right and wrong is less clearly defined than previously. Religion and authorities in general do not carry the force they once did, leaving the way more open for brands to be ideas to live our lives by. This also goes with the thirst for a new sense of heritage and authenticity, an interest in origin and depth.

The dissolution of social structures and a fixed pattern to life means that brands can play with the sense of where they fit or might be used. Treats do not need to be saved for a Sunday or a special occasion. Equally, it means you should be careful over promoting the longevity of your brand. A statement that the brand has been around for 50 years runs an increasing risk of implying that it's out of date. Stability now needs to be a more flexible concept – evolution on a dependable theme, contrasted to revolution, which would be the hallmark of brands pushing the opposite need of curiosity.

Physical World (Structure)

The need for a physical groundedness is emphasised as a counterbalance to the freedoms encouraged by technology and changes in social structure. It means an emphasis on body consciousness and the physical senses, exemplified by the growth in appreciation of food – not just enjoyment of food, but awareness of its quality and provenance. It's a recognition that the quality of life is rooted in the physical body and the way you take care of it. You can see it in things such as the growing awareness of the dangers of crash diets, or too much exposure to the sun.

Obviously a whole range of food, drink and personal care products and services have to take this trend into account, even if they don't actively try to exploit it. The phrase 'a little of what you fancy does you good' is as true as ever, but as a brand you just have to be clever about how you use it.

Another theme connected with structure is the loss of routine, through the growth of jobs involving lots of travel, or home working, or flexible hours. It means you're less likely to know where you are going to be and what you will be doing, hence the appeal of electronic organisers and diaries. People still need routine, but they need to find positive expressions of it, since it is increasingly viewed as something negative. There should be lots of opportunities for brands here.

Speed and Efficiency (Practicality)

Everything is happening faster and faster. And indeed, the services company mantra 'faster, better, cheaper' makes it clear the energy that is put in to propel this progress. Perhaps, therefore, this has always been with us, but the standards are now higher. People will always listen to the claim 'gets it done in half the time' to try to save time in their hectic lives. Of course, mathematically, you can keep halving the time again and again without limit.

The stakes seem to be higher now, as increasing numbers of people become cash rich but time poor. So if you can find a way of helping those people theoretically release a little time, they will buy your product in the belief it will help them. It doesn't really matter to your brand that what they will do with the extra time is likely to be rush around trying to get more cash rich.

Part of the undertow is the risk of doubts about quality. For instance, there are many movements promoting the benefits of 'slow food', but they don't yet seem to have seriously dented the sales of fast food. The higher stakes that come with modern speed seem to mean that when something goes wrong it drives us absolutely mad. Or, as someone described using a computer: 'It's like driving a car very fast, but then coming to a terrifying, instant halt each time the computer crashes'. We are more impatient, and the contrast between normal service and breakdown has become more marked.

New Status and Achievement (Challenge)

As we find with many of the other trend areas, the question of status is becoming a lot more complex and fluid. There seems to be simultaneous abandonment of old forms, such as office dress codes, as well as a thirst for new guidance rushing to fill the gap. Connected to this is Andy Warhol's idea of fifteen minutes of fame for everyone, increasingly achievable through reality TV shows. Now anyone can be famous.

The concept of status and achievement remain, but they have become more personal, individual and private. Overt status symbols are likely to be less successful than more thoughtful ones. Brands need more to be a help to people trying to fulfil their personal ambitions, whether improving their golf, or fighting off their heavy cold so they can carry on at work.

Customer power is another aspect of change in the notion of challenge. People expect to be able to ask challenging questions and make complaints. The company or brand is no longer on an unassailable pedestal; it is available for one-to-one discussions and even arguments.

Do Your Own Thing (Self-expression)

The notion of a brand as something fixed and unchanging is receding, as is the insistence of 'one size fits all'. We've gone from Henry Ford's 'any colour so long as it's black', through 'many colours to choose from', through to 'create your own colour'.

Customisation is thus a big trend, with many brands such as Egg or PlayStation putting the consumer in a position of power. You know you're in charge if you are the one who is making all the choices. It brings an added sense of responsibility and a feeling of challenge. This trend is easy to see for services brands, but you might not expect it for packaged goods. Yet you might include in this area such simple things as split-pot yoghurts or salad bars in supermarkets, where you fill a tub with your own choices from the selection available.

People have always wanted independence, but now services respond in a wider variety of ways to deal with this. The rise of telephone and Internet banking is a good example: this is more than just a time-saver, it encourages a feeling of independence.

Living Life (Excitement)

A theme throughout this text has been the growth in brands as complete experiences, and a 'try it and see' approach by consumers. It relates to greater consumer confidence in brand switching and risk taking, an idea caught by the Rolling Rock brand of beer in its advertising. More broadly it is a push towards deeper quality of life through the richness of leisure experiences, a world of excitement and possibility.

There are no barriers. Almost anyone can think of going anywhere and doing anything, if they wish to, and any brand involved with travel or leisure pursuits has the opportunity to tap into these themes. Virtual reality technology will increasingly create new possibilities for experience.

Technology and Wide Horizons (Curiosity)

New technology may well be the first trend that someone would name spontaneously. For many people it is a personal interest, and appropriate brands can catch this trend directly. As with many things, there is a leading edge and a second wave. The leading edge products and brands are the province of the few, and are often visibly exciting because they are so new they are prone to going wrong! As someone once said, 'If it works every time you don't think of it as new technology'. When these products settle down, they become more reliable and reach a wider second wave, also with a genuine but a less dynamic interest in technology.

Under the heading of 'Small Planet' we talked about the growth of caring concerns through a wider sense of community. Here, the same trend towards global awareness fuels opportunities to discover new things, without having to identify with your fellow human beings. The recent media explosion – 100 TV channels instead of three or four, and information about any place or subject at the touch of a computer key – has fuelled a worldwide thirst for information.

The underlying need, or drive, is to look around the next corner and see what's there. The modern world gives you many ways of doing this, and doing it more quickly.

Freedom of Identity (Liberty)

Today, we are less and less defined by our demographics: the statement 'I am a thirty-five-year-old married man' says less than it used to about our place in life, our interests and activities. Divisions between masculine and feminine roles are reducing; for example, men will happily admit to reading women's magazines or being a house husband. In terms of age, a motto for new attitudes would be, 'You're never too old to…'. This freedom is particularly evident among the over-40s or 50s, a group increasing in number and in health, and not feeling middle-aged or old.

The classic life stages used to be defined as dependent, pre-family, family, post-family and retired. Notice the emphasis on family and your position before, during or after it. These seem less relevant now in understanding people, although admittedly the family stage when you first have young children can still override everything.

The lesson for brands in one way is very simple. Forget demographics, life stages and typical household situations. Instead, work on needs that any person can tap into, regardless of who they are. Your brand could help people think differently about themselves, catching that sense of liberty.

The Future for Brands

Brands are now entwined in our lives as never before, and this is reflected in our expectations of them and the ways we relate to them. The most successful ones are those that fit closely with our current needs, our changing society, that deal with us honestly and personally, and that act as positive partners in living life.

Modern brands provide all the benefits of their ancestors: emotional and practical reassurance about doing the job, a hook for achievement, a vehicle for self-expression and aspiration, and a means of self-exploration. Our demands have forced them to concentrate on their authenticity, to adapt and to grow with us.

We are coming through the explosion of choice to a time of consolidation into fewer brands, but where each brand has a more flexible identity, stretching across and within categories. While the overcrowding and dominance of a relatively small number of giant companies might seem to limit opportunities, in fact there are always new brands appearing, or reappearing. The fundamental human needs, on which brands are based, are constant but progressing, always with fresh opportunities.

The underlying patterns have always been there, but they shift and evolve.

Index